Goal planning with elderly people

How to make plans to meet an individual's needs

A manual of instruction

CHRISTINE BARROWCLOUGH
IAN FLEMING

Manchester University Press

Published by Manchester University Press
Oxford Road, Manchester M13 9PL, UK
and 51 Washington Street, Dover,
New Hampshire 03820, USA

British Library cataloguing in publication data

Barrowclough, Christine
    Goal-planning with elderly people: how to
    make plans to meet an individual's needs: a
    manual of instruction.
    1. Geriatric psychiatry   2. Goal (Psychology)
    I. Title   II. Fleming, Ian
    362.2'1'0880565   RC451.4.A5

Library of Congress cataloging in publication data

Barrowclough, Christine
    Goal planning with elderly people.
    1. Social work with the aged.   2. Aged – Services for.
I. Fleming, Ian.   II. Title
HV1451.B37   1985   362.6'042   85–7120

ISBN 0 7190 1802 1 (*paperback*)

Printed and Typeset in Times New Roman and Univers on MCS5/8300
by Elliott Bros. & Yeoman Ltd., Woodend Avenue, Speke, Liverpool L24 9JL

Contents

Acknowledgements

The authors wish to acknowledge that the term and techniques of *goal planning* were introduced by Peter Houts and Robert Scott (1975)[1] in their work with developmentally disabled children. This manual has attempted to modify and adopt their procedures for work with elderly people.

We would like to thank our colleague, Bob Whitmore, for his assistance in this work. Also the staff, volunteers, and clients at Age Concern Day Centre in Swinton, Salford who helped us to test our original materials, and in particular June Guthrie.

The work was part of a project funded by the Mental Health Foundation.

[1]Houts, P. S. and Scott, R. A. (1975). *Goal planning with developmentally disabled persons: procedures for developing an individualised client plan*. Pennsylvania, Milton Hershey Medical Center.

Introduction

This manual contains information that will help you in your work with elderly people. The purpose of the manual is to assist you in acquiring the skills to work out individual plans for elderly clients. It is designed for you to use under the guidance of someone who is already familiar with the techniques of *goal planning*. Appendix IV contains notes for an instructor to carry this out.

The best way to learn new skills is by trying to put them into practice. We have designed the manual with this aim in mind. It is divided into eleven sections. For the most part, each section gives you information about some aspect of the process of *goal planning*. This is followed by a series of examples and exercises, allowing you to try out the techniques with clients and gain expertise.

Included in the manual are master blank copies of the forms used in the goal planning process. You are encouraged to copy these, **but no other parts of the manual**, for use in practice after completing your training.

When you have completed all the work contained in the manual, you will have the skills to:

(a) identify the exact and individual needs of elderly people;
(b) design and carry out programmes which will enable those needs to be met;
(c) evaluate the effectiveness of these programmes and change them if necessary.

Appendix III at the back of the manual gives you a complete example of how this is done, from first principles, using the techniques of *goal planning*.

It may be thought that elderly clients who are 'confused' or who are diagnosed to have neurological difficulties such as 'memory problems', 'apraxias', 'agnosias' and so on may not be able to benefit from *goal planning*. Our experience, and that of staff trained by us in *goal planning* techniques, has not lent support to this view. We feel this is largely because *goal planning* is not a 'cookbook' approach to behaviour which is applied generally, irrespective of any individual client's particular ability or disabilities. On the contrary, *goal planning* of necessity involves an assessment of the individual's strengths and needs and any *goal plan* devised properly will use this information directly. The consideration of all relevant information about the person in formulating the *goal plan*, and the procedures for protecting against the person failing repeatedly on the steps towards the goal are particular assets of the approach. These are not so apparent in other therapeutic formulations which either separate assessment from intervention, or do not use the assessment information to decide how the client's abilities, disabilities and their environment will affect the intervention.

Thus, we feel that the disabilities, or reduced level of ability (or strength), represented by 'confused' states or neurological difficulties will be fully taken into consideration when *goal planning*. Any *goal plans* formulated for neurologically impaired clients may, therefore, reduce the speed at which help given to the client is faded out, or increase the range of cues, or reminders, placed in the environment to encourage the client's behaviour to take place. *Goal planning* is an individualised way of formulating plans to help elderly clients. Because of this we do not feel that its usage can be discounted in advance for certain clients. Notwithstanding this, however, we would, of course, advise any clients to be in physical good health before embarking on *goal planning* and a physician's advice should be sought if necessary.

SECTION 1

Assessment and observation

1.1 In order to make plans to help an elderly person, we need to know just what a person can do, and what sort of things are a problem to them.

This is called making an *assessment* of the person's strengths and needs. This assessment is a central part of making the *goal plan* which will try to meet the elderly person's needs.

One important part of making the assessment is careful *observation*. In this first section we will discuss what this means in practice, and show you how to go about making careful observations.

1.2 Observation

The basis of any assessment of human behaviour must be observation. For example, if we wish to know how well a person is able to handle money, the best assessment will be to observe how well a person performs in a variety of situations, e.g. adding coins together to pay for goods in a shop, checking the money given to them for their pension at the Post Office. Although we might feel we know a person well, we cannot be sure that they can do things unless we confirm behaviours by observation. In the example above you may feel that a client is able to handle money because they seem to be very competent in other ways, e.g. they can hold an interesting conversation and make a good cup of tea. However, unless you actually *observe* other aspects of their behaviour you will not know for certain what they can and can't do. Another important reason for observation is to give you a picture of how well a person is able to do an activity *before* you attempt to change it. By taking a measure of the person's behaviour at this stage it is possible to see whether your intervention will lead to any change later on.

1.3 Making observations

Clearly, those who spend a good deal of time with a person have the best opportunity to make observations. However, there are problems in making such observations:

(a) How do you decide what to include? Of all the behaviours that take place during the day, which are significant and worthy of note?

(b) People who spend a lot of time with the person to be assessed can be so familiar or close to the person that they may overlook important aspects of behaviour. One tends to 'see' what one expects. It is sometimes difficult, therefore, to stand back and examine the behaviour afresh.

(c) One may have become accustomed to doing things for a person, and consequently assume that they cannot do these things for themselves. Only by standing back and observing them doing things without help will you be able to assess what they can do independently.

1.4 Making reliable observations

It is important to make observations that are reliable. The reliability of observations refers to how consistent they are: that is, the extent to which two or more people can agree on the occurrence of whatever it is being observed.

This can be more difficult than it at first sounds. Reliable observation is a skill which must be acquired through practice. We have to become more objective, to look carefully, and avoid jumping to conclusions before they are justified. You may be surprised to discover how difficult it is to achieve complete agreement. It is well known that witnesses to a car accident frequently give very different versions of what happened. The following example and exercises will help you to understand these points.

Before looking at example **1.6**, there a few points which you need to bear in mind.

1. Two people can 'see' different things when watching the same sequence of behaviours.
2. It is important to decide in advance what aspects of behaviour you are interested in, and to *define* or pinpoint these clearly.
3. Having a clear definition of behaviour helps to obtain reliable information.
4. A clear definition is one which any two people would agree on.

1.5   Example of how people can disagree about a client's behaviour unless they *define clearly* what it is, and carefully *observe* the behaviour

Sue and Joan are care staff in an elderly persons' home. The home has decided to introduce tea-making facilities for the clients to use when they wish. Sue and Joan disagree about how much help a resident, Mrs Kelly, requires to make a pot of tea. Sue says Mrs Kelly 'needs a lot of help' from staff; Joan says Mrs Kelly 'only needs a bit of help'. Whose opinion is correct? What do the phrases 'a lot of help' and 'a bit of help' mean?

To resolve matters Sue and Joan decide to *pinpoint* or *clearly define* the main *behaviours* involved in making a pot of tea. They draw up a *record sheet* on which to note down these behaviours, and how much help Mrs Kelly requires to perform each of them. They break down 'how much help' into:

> no help
> verbal prompts
> physical prompts
> unable to do

They ask Mrs Kelly's permission to observe her making a pot of tea. They decide to observe her on two occasions, because her behaviour can sometimes vary. They record their observations on the record sheet they have prepared.

1.6 Example of pinpointing, observing and recording a client's behaviour

PINPOINTING AND OBSERVING A CLIENT'S BEHAVIOUR

Behaviour to be observed: Mrs Kelly making a pot of tea

When and where: In the kitchen at the home on Wednesday and Thursday afternoons

Observers: Sue and Joan

Behaviours to be observed	Observer: Sue				Observer: Sue			
	Date: Wednesday 8th November				Date: Thursday 9th November			
	No help	Verbal prompt	Physical prompt	Unable to do	No help	Verbal prompt	Physical prompt	Unable to do
1. Filling the kettle	✓				✓			
2. Plugging in kettle/switching on			✓			✓		
3. Warming pot		✓				✓		
4. Putting tea in pot	✓					✓		
5. Switching off kettle when boiled/ pouring water into pot	✓				✓			

PINPOINTING AND OBSERVING A CLIENT'S BEHAVIOUR

Behaviour to be observed: Mrs Kelly making a pot of tea

When and where: In the kitchen at the home on Wednesday and Thursday afternoons

Observers: Sue and Joan

Behaviours to be observed	Observer: Joan				Observer: Joan			
	Date: Wednesday 8th November				Date: Thursday 9th November			
	No help	Verbal prompt	Physical prompt	Unable to do	No help	Verbal prompt	Physical prompt	Unable to do
1. Filling the kettle	✓				✓			
2. Plugging in kettle/switching on		✓					✓	
3. Warming pot		✓				✓		
4. Putting tea in pot	✓				✓			
5. Switching off kettle when boiled/ pouring water into pot		✓			✓			

1.7 Exercise in making conclusions about the recorded observations in 1.6

Some questions:

(a) Which observations were reliable?

                                                        reliable   unreliable

1. Filling the kettle
2. Plugging in kettle/switching on
3. Warming pot
4. Putting tea in pot
5. Switching off kettle, etc.

(b) Can you suggest any reasons why the observers sometimes reported 'seeing' different things?

(c) You are going to try and improve Mrs Kelly's ability to make a pot of tea. From the observations recorded in **1.6** what would you conclude Mrs Kelly *can do now,* before you begin to help her to be more independent?

1.8 Some answers to the questions in exercise 1.7

(a) Which observations were reliable?

	reliable	unreliable
1. Filling the kettle	✔	
2. Plugging in kettle/switching on		✔
3. Warming pot	✔	
4. Putting tea in pot		✔
5. Switching off kettle, etc.		✔

The observations can be concluded to be *reliable* when *both* observers agreed *exactly* on *both* occasions that they observed.

(b) Why did the observers sometimes report 'seeing' different things? Possibly due to:

- lapses in concentration
- different expectations about what Mrs Kelly could do
- uncertainty about what is a *verbal prompt* and what is a *physical prompt*

It is a good idea to sort out what you mean by 'verbal' and 'physical' prompts before you begin to observe. As a guideline a *verbal prompt* is spoken help, reminder or instruction; a *physical prompt* is physical guidance.

(c) *Conclusions* Mrs Kelly can fill the kettle without help. She needs verbal prompts to warm the pot, put the tea in the pot, switch off the kettle and pour in the water. She needs physical prompts to plug in the kettle.

If there is *some doubt* about a client's abilities, even after careful observation, assume you will have to begin trying to improve behaviour from the lowest level you have observed. It is better to *underestimate* than to overestimate, since you want to ensure that you do not set your goals too high. If you do the person may experience failure.

1.9 Exercise in pinpointing and observing a client's behaviour

Decide on a client and an aspect of their behaviour you wish to observe. Pinpoint and write down exactly what you will observe. Try and get someone to observe and record the behaviour with you so you can check the *reliability* of your observations. (N.B. ask the client's permission *before* you observe) Note down your conclusions on the next page.

PINPOINTING AND OBSERVING A CLIENT'S BEHAVIOUR

Behaviour to be observed

When and where

Observers

Behaviours to be observed	Observer				Observer			
	Date				Date			
	No help	Verbal prompt	Physical prompt	Unable to do	No help	Verbal prompt	Physical prompt	Unable to do
1								
2								
3								
4								
5								
6								
7								
8								

1.10   Conclusions from exercise 1.9

(a) Which observations were reliable?

	reliable	*unreliable*
1		
2		
3		
4		
5		
6		
7		
8		

(b) Can you suggest any reasons why you and your second observer reported 'seeing' different things?

SECTION 2

Using the Elderly Person's Assessment Charts

2.1 In Section 1 we said that an essential part of preparing to help your elderly client was to observe his or her behaviour. An important part of making this assessment is the skill of being able to *clearly define or pinpoint* the behaviours you wish to observe.

This second section is concerned with building up your assessment of the client's behaviour. It shows you how to complete the Elderly Person's Assessment Charts, a copy of which is contained in Appendix 1 at the back of the manual.

2.2 The assessment charts

We have already discussed some of the difficulties which may arise in observing people's behaviour. We have also pointed out that the observation and assessment is made easier and more reliable if we know in advance what items of behaviour to look for.

For this reason we have compiled the Assessment Charts. These will help you to look closely at important aspects of an elderly person's behaviour. The behaviours listed in the charts are important for elderly people in terms of their independent functioning, ability to cope and well-being. Therefore, with the help of the charts you can begin to build up a picture of what they can do and what they have difficulty with. This will help in making plans of how to try and meet their needs.

2.3 What the charts contain

The charts are divided into two sections. Each section covers different aspects of behaviour, and also requires a different method of completion. The two sections are as follows:

Section 1

(a) Sensory abilities: eyesight
                                   hearing

(b) Mobility: walking
                                   stairs
                                   ability to get out of house
                                   frequency of leaving the house

(c) Social contact

Section 2

(a) Personal self-help skills: dressing–undressing
                                          selection of clothing
                                        use of toilet
                                         personal hygiene
                                         eating

(*b*) Domestic self-help skills: washing clothes
                                                                 cooking
                                                                 housework, etc.
(*c*) Shopping and handling money
(*d*) Communication
(*e*) Occupation
(*f*) First aid and health
(*g*) Orientation and memory

2.4   How to complete the charts

In Appendix II at the back of the manual there is a detailed description of each of the sections of the charts. This discusses the importance of the items in the section, and gives some guidelines on how to assess the items. It is important to read this Appendix *before* you begin to fill in the charts with your client.

Basically, there are three ways of collecting the information you need to fill in the charts:

1. *Ask* the client.
2. *Observe* the client.
3. *Ask* other people who know the client well, for example, relatives, friends or neighbours.

As we learnt in Section 1, the best way of finding out about human behaviour is by observing it. Try to complete the charts by using information about what you have *seen* the client do whenever possible.

However, often it will be impossible to do this since you will not have had the opportunity to observe some of the things listed in the charts. It will then be necessary to *ask* the client about things. Most often it will also be necessary to ask someone else who knows the client well. Sometimes there will be disagreement between what the *client* says he or she is able to do, and what the *relative or friend* says the client can do. In such a case it is important to try and *observe* the client doing the task yourself. It is essential that you *always* observe the behaviour that you decide to focus on in your goal plan.

2.5 Exercise

Select a client that you wish to work with using *goal planning*.

   Complete the Elderly Person's Assessment Charts on this client, and fill in the comments section below.

Name of client

Names of other people giving information about the client

	Comments about completing the charts, e.g. difficulties, reliability and so on.
1. Information from client	
2. Information from others	
3. Own observations	

2.6 Summary

So far we have concentrated on the importance of observation and assessment to successful *goal planning*. We have emphasised:

    (*a*) the need for clear and reliable observations of clients' actual behaviour

    (*b*) pinpointing the behaviour which you wish to observe

    (*c*) using the Assessment Charts to make assessments of a client's behaviour in specific areas

This assessment information will be of great help to you in building up a picture of your client's skills. The ability to make accurate and reliable observations is essential to be able to use *goal planning*. In the next section we will look at the way to make a specific assessment of your client which will be the first stage in developing a *goal plan*.

SECTION 3

Using the strengths–needs list

3.1 Having made an assessment of your client using the assessment chart described in the previous chapter, you will now have a great deal of information about the client. The next step towards devising an action plan, is to work out a *strengths–needs list*. This helps you in several ways.

Firstly, it is often the case that when we look at the problems an elderly person faces, we forget the *positive* things about that person i.e. his/her *strengths*. As we shall see, discovering what a client's strengths are can be vitally important when we come to working out a treatment plan.

Secondly, when you are looking at the sort of assistance an elderly person requires, it is all too easy to think about his/her problems *negatively*. That is, you may tend to look at their difficulties in terms of what they can't do. For example, you may write 'Mrs Brown cannot feed herself properly'. When filling in a strengths–needs list, you should rewrite this positively to make it a *need*, i.e., 'Mrs Brown needs to learn to feed herself'. This second statement directs you towards working out a plan to help Mrs Brown feed herself. The first statement is negative, and doesn't direct you anywhere.

3.2 What are strengths?

There are three sorts of strengths:

- What the client *can* do
- What the client *likes* to do
- People who would be willing to *help*

(i) *What the client can do* Under 'strengths' you should list all the most important things the client can do. For example, a client may be able to walk quite well, so you could write 'Mr Smith can walk up to a quarter of a mile without much difficulty'. It would be very useful to have this information if one of the needs for Mr Smith was to increase his social activities. (When you are listing the things the client can do, it may not be clear how some things could be useful – you should write them down anyway, as it is only when you have completed the whole strengths–needs list that you may see how strengths could be used to help meet needs.)

(ii) *What the client likes to do* These are important strengths, as preferences, hobbies, interests, etc. can be an important part of a plan. For example, a client's strength could be 'Mrs Jones likes to have a cup of tea with her neighbour Mrs Davis', and she also has a *need* to be able to walk more confidently. You can link these two together so that Mrs Jones is helped (as little help as is necessary) to Mrs Davis' each morning for a cup of tea and a chat.

You should also include old interests and hobbies, which the client no longer does. For example, if you have a client who is very depressed, but used to enjoy dancing (a strength), then you might want to include old time dancing socials as a strategy to help him become more active and so overcome the depression. Your client's willingness to be involved in the *goal plan* can also be included as a significant strength.

(iii) *People who would be willing to help*   It is very useful to know if there are any people who are acquainted with the client who may be willing to help in any way in carrying out a treatment plan. For example, if a client has a friend and a neighbour who are both willing to help, then you could arrange that each gets involved in a treatment plan, sharing what they have to do together. The fact that they already know the client may make the plan much easier to carry out.

3.3   How do you find out a client's strengths?

(i)   *Ask the client*   If your client can talk, s/he will be able to tell you a lot about what they like doing (and used to like doing), and who they like and trust. If you know what your client likes to do, you know what they'll be *motivated* to do.

(ii)   *Ask people who are significantly involved with the client*   Family, friends and neighbours who know the client, will almost certainly have important information to give you about your client's strengths. You will also discover to what extent these people will be willing to help in a treatment plan.

(iii)   *Use the Assessment Chart, and your own observations*   The Assessment Chart will give you a lot of information as to what the client can do, and this will provide you with a number of strengths to include in the list, as well as strengths discovered from your own observations not included in the chart.

3.4   What are needs?

Needs are the problems your client faces restated *in positive terms.* For example, rather than stating that 'Mr Jones should stop walking around with his trousers undone', it is far better to write: 'Mr Jones needs to learn to do his trousers up'. It is better to write needs in this positive way – what the client needs to *do*, not what he should *stop* doing – because you are making it clear what has to be done to help meet the client's need. Writing 'Mr Jones should stop walking around with his trousers undone' does not help you in this way. At the end of this section there is an exercise for you to do which will help you to write your client's needs positively.

3.5   How do you find out a client's needs?

(i)   *Ask the client*   Your client may be able to tell you a good deal about the problems s/he is facing. S/he may be able to give you additional information about needs you have already discovered. For example, if a client who is incontinent tells you that s/he knows when s/he wants to go, but just can't get to the toilet in time, then this information will be very helpful in writing down the need more accurately.

The client may also inform you of needs which you had not observed. For example, a client may inform you that s/he feels very anxious about going out in case s/he falls over. Again this will be useful information.

If you know what the client sees as his/her main needs, you will be able to devise plans that are more personally relevant to the client.

(ii) *Ask people who are significantly involved with the client* Family, friends and neighbours will almost certainly be able to give you information about the client's needs, having seen the client in a number of different situations where difficulties may arise, for example, shopping. You will also find out what these people have already been doing to help meet the client's needs, and this information may be very useful.

(iii) *Use the Assessment Chart and your own observations* The Assessment Chart will have a great deal of information about those areas in which the client is having problems, for example, in dressing, or in mobility. This information will also be quite detailed, in that you will know the extent of the need, and the assistance necessary. For example, if the client has a problem dressing, you will know to what extent she can already dress herself and where there are specific needs, such as in doing up buttons. This information can be readily restated in positive terms on the strengths-needs list.

   You may also have noted other needs not included in the assessment Chart, and these should be included as well.

3.6   Summary: *the strengths-needs list*

The *strengths-needs list* is useful for two main reasons:

(i) It enables all the positive things about the client to be taken into account, that is the client's *strengths*. Strengths include the things the client can do, things the client likes to do, and people who are willing to help.

(ii) The *strengths-needs list* allows you to summarise the main areas of need from the chart (and other sources). These are restated in *positive* terms, that is, what the client needs to be doing, not what s/he should *stop* doing. This helps you plan more effectively to meet the client's needs.

3.7   Example of a strengths–needs list completed for a client named Arthur

STRENGTHS–NEEDS LIST

Client	Date

Strengths	**Needs**
What the individual can do, what s/he likes to do, and other people who are willing to help	State these positively – what s/he should be doing
● Likes talking to staff	● Needs to increase his social contact
● Knows and recognises people in local shops	● Needs to have more occupational interests
● Able to buy small things in shops	● Needs to improve his personal hygiene
● Knows way around local neighbourhood	● Needs to use hearing aid more regularly
● Likes a drink (beer)	● Needs to be able to make hot snacks for self
● Has good eyesight	
● Can make a cup of tea/coffee for self	
● Can make cold snacks, e.g. sandwiches	
● Is willing to participate in *goal planning*	
● Can do hand-washing when reminded	
● Can read the paper and enjoys doing so	
● Likes to keep in touch with his family	
● Can shave self when reminded	

3.8 Exercise on how to state needs in positive terms

Remember that we are constructing a *strengths–needs* assessment to find out what the client needs help with. We are therefore concentrating on what the client needs to be doing in future.

We will find this much easier if we state the client's needs in *positive* terms. Below are two lists of behaviours for a fictional client. Those on the right-hand side are stated in positive terms. They give us much more idea of what we need to be doing. Finish off the list so that all those on the left-hand side are restated in more positive terms.

WRONG!!!	CORRECT!!!
Things Colin cannot do – stated in negative terms	*Things Colin needs to be able to do – stated in positive terms*
● He is unfriendly	● He needs to become more friendly and sociable
● He is dirty	● He needs to develop his washing skills
● He is bored and uninterested	● He needs to find a new range of stimulating interests
● He can't cook for himself	
● He makes a mess when drinking from a cup or glass	
● He mumbles	
● He is selfish and won't join in	
● He is scruffy	

3.9   Exercise in writing a strengths–needs list for your client

Pick a client who you know well and are likely to be working with. She or he will probably be the same person for whom you have already completed the Assessment Charts in Section 2. From your knowledge of the person and his or her situation make a list of strengths and needs. If you feel it helps, ask others (e.g. relatives, neighbours) who know the client well, and observe the client's actual behaviour yourself.

STRENGTHS–NEEDS LIST

Client	Date

Strengths	**Needs**
What the individual can do, what s/he likes to do, and other people who are willing to help	State these positively – what s/he should be doing

SECTION 4
Selecting one of the client's needs to work with

4.1 Having now completed a *strengths–needs list* on your client you will have (i) a list of the person's *strengths* and (ii) another list containing the *needs* stated in positive terms. Later on we will be using the information contained in the Strengths list to help us formulate a plan with which we can help the client attain one of his or her needs.

4.2 However, before we do this we must choose one from the list of *needs* to work with, and write this as a *goal* or target for the individual to achieve. In the next section we will show you how to write your chosen need as a *goal*. Before that we will look at how you make your choice of the need to work with.

4.3 Your client will have a number of needs with which you could be of help. However, it is best to make only one plan at a time and therefore you must select one need from the list. In making this choice you should follow these guidelines:

(i)   The client should be involved as much as possible in making the decision. At the very least, you should explain as fully as possible the goal that you have selected and will be making a plan for.

(ii)   You should choose a need which is important to the *client*. This may seem obvious and not worth mentioning, but sometimes it is easy to pick a need that helps the institution the client lives in, or the staff or other elderly people rather than the client him or herself. Always remember when selecting a need that the interests of the client come first.

(iii)   Choose a need for which you think there is a good chance of success. There is no extra value in attempting to meet the most difficult of the client's needs just for the sake of it.

(iv)   Especially at first, choose a need with which you think you will have success in the short-term (say five or six weeks). Later, when you've had more practice at *goal planning* and feel more confident, you can attempt to develop longer-term plans.

When you have made your choice, this need will then become the *goal* of the plan which you will make for the elderly client you are working with. In the rest of this section we will look at examples of selecting needs for clients.

4.4   Example of selecting one of a client's needs to work with

Mr Farmer attends a day centre for elderly people. Staff completed a *strengths–needs list* on him and, as can be seen, he has quite a few needs. The staff of the day centre discussed these and decided to help meet only one of these needs for the following reasons:

Mr Farmer's *needs*:
- to speak more clearly
- to remember to use his hearing aid
- to remember to take his prescribed medicine more regularly
- to improve his personal hygiene
- to make snacks for himself
- to manage small purchases for himself
- to judge when food needs to be eaten and how long it will last for

Need selected as *goal* to work towards:

Mr Farmer will wear his hearing aid and have it switched on at all times when attending the day centre

Reasons for selecting this *need*:

- Staff felt that Mr Farmer would be able to achieve the *goal* fairly quickly
- Staff felt that if Mr Farmer couldn't hear people, it would be harder for him to begin to meet some of his other needs. It was therefore a priority for him
- In discussion with staff Mr Farmer agreed that he would like to be able to remember to use his hearing aid properly
- Staff felt pretty confident that they could achieve this goal and judged that their success on this would help them work on more difficult *goals* later

4.5 Exercise in selecting a need from the strengths–needs list

1. Look back to the *strengths–needs list* which you completed in the last session.
2. Select *one* need from the list to work with using the guidelines just discussed.
3. Give the reasons why you selected the need in the space below:

SELECTING A NEED FROM THE STRENGTHS–NEEDS LIST
Name of client
Need selected to work on
Reasons for selecting the need

SECTION 5

Rewriting the need chosen for your client as a clear goal

5.1   Up until now we have been satisfied to describe a client's needs in quite general, everyday terms. As we get closer to formulating our plan for changing the client's behaviour we will have to become more specific. When we re-write the need which has been chosen for the client as a *goal*, we must describe exactly what the client will be doing when the need has been met. We must refer to the client's behaviour and do so in very clear terms. Exercises 5.2 and 5.3 will give you practice in doing this.

In addition to stating the client's *goal* in clear behavioural language, when we come to write the *goal-plan* it will help us to know what the client's present level of behaviour is. This will help us to see how much behaviour change is required for the *goal* (and therefore the client's original Need) to be achieved. When the *goal plan* is put together, both the client's present and target behaviours need to be written down in clear behavioural terms which describe *who* is doing or will do *what, when* and *how*.

5.2   Exercise in rewriting your chosen need as a clear goal

STATING CHOSEN NEED AS A CLEAR GOAL
Name of client
NEED which you have chosen to work on with your client
Clear GOAL for your client to meet

5.3   Exercise in writing clear goals

When writing goals it is important to remember 3 points:

1. The goal should be stated *positively*.
2. The goal should pinpoint the *behaviour* of the client.
3. The goal should be stated clearly. The clearest way to write a goal is to describe what the *client* will be doing when the goal is achieved.

Below is an exercise in using clear language when writing goals. the goals on the left-hand side of the page are too vague. Try and rewrite the goals clearly in the space on the right-hand side, as in the example given.

Vague goals

Clear goals

Mr Smith will socialise more.

Mr Smith will participate in a game of cards each day he attends

Mr Jones will improve his personal hygiene.

Mrs Smith will dress properly.

Mr Hill will go out more.

Miss Davies will do some shopping.

Mrs Moore will be less dependant on other people.

Mr Barnes will improve his eating habits.

Mrs Harris will occupy herself more.

Mr Cox will stop demanding attention.

Miss Campbell will speak better.

SECTION 6

Developing approaches for helping the client meet his or her need

6.1 One of the great advantages of the *goal-planning* approach is the way that it comes together as a complete system for helping us to meet the needs of elderly clients. If we carefully complete a *strengths–needs list* on an individual client, taking care to accurately observe the person's behaviour and needs, we will have almost all the information necessary to write a *goal-plan* for the person concerned.

So far in this manual we have assessed the client using the *strengths–needs list* and selected an important need to work on. We know that this need is the *goal* for which we will later be writing a *plan,* but as yet we haven't started to do so.

In this section we will make a start on this by using the list of strengths to help us develop a number of practical approaches which we can later build into our plan. You will be able to see that a good *strengths–needs list* provides most of the important information necessary for this.

To do so, look at the strengths list and write down all of the possible ways that you could use the client's strengths to help him or her reach the goal that you have decided on. Review each strength and write down as many ideas as you can as to how these could be used. Don't worry if some of these seem slightly fanciful or unrealistic, you can always leave them out later, but at this stage you should generate as many ideas as possible. We will use the most practical to form the *goal-plan.* (See Fig. 1.)

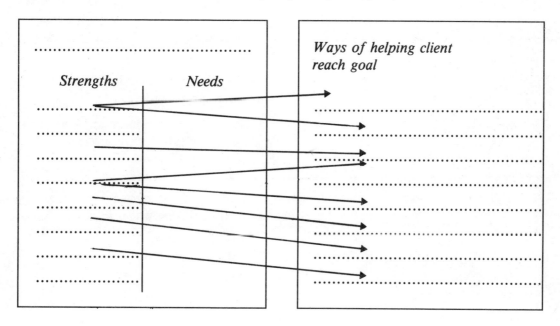

Figure 1

6.2   Example of using a client's strengths to make a list of ways for helping the client reach his or her goal

Mr Hart attends a day centre and has a variety of needs, mainly to do with getting out and socialising more. The staff at the day centre have compiled a *strengths–needs list* on Mr Hart and chosen the following need to work on and rewritten it as a *goal*:

GOAL: Mr Hart will visit his friend in the next street twice a week.

Below are some of Mr Hart's behaviours (from the strengths list) and the ideas that staff developed from these for possible use in making the *GOAL-PLAN* which they will later write to help meet Mr Hart's need. They may decide only to use some of these ideas, but developing these approaches has helped them in looking at how they might begin to write the *goal-plan*.

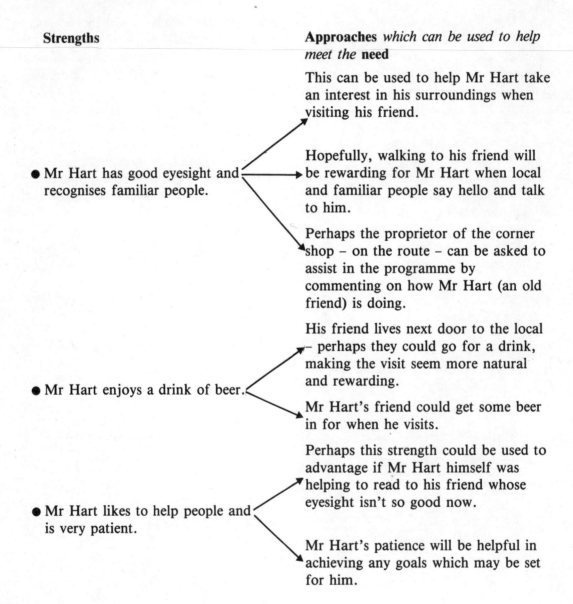

Strengths

Approaches *which can be used to help meet the* **need**

This can be used to help Mr Hart take an interest in his surroundings when visiting his friend.

● Mr Hart has good eyesight and recognises familiar people.

Hopefully, walking to his friend will be rewarding for Mr Hart when local and familiar people say hello and talk to him.

Perhaps the proprietor of the corner shop – on the route – can be asked to assist in the programme by commenting on how Mr Hart (an old friend) is doing.

His friend lives next door to the local – perhaps they could go for a drink, making the visit seem more natural and rewarding.

● Mr Hart enjoys a drink of beer.

Mr Hart's friend could get some beer in for when he visits.

Perhaps this strength could be used to advantage if Mr Hart himself was helping to read to his friend whose eyesight isn't so good now.

● Mr Hart likes to help people and is very patient.

Mr Hart's patience will be helpful in achieving any goals which may be set for him.

6.3 Exercise on using a client's strengths to make a list of ways for helping the client to reach his or her goal

Below is some information about a client called Mrs McBrien. A goal has been chosen for her and a list of some of the strengths from her *strengths–needs list* is also included. Use these to develop some ways which you could use to help Mrs McBrien reach her *goal*. *Think about* how you could usefully use the information contained in the strengths.

GOAL: Mrs McBrien will dress herself in indoor clothes, independently and in the correct order every day.

Strengths	**Approaches** *which can be used to help meet the* **need**
● Mrs McBrien has a good grip. ⟶	
● Mrs McBrien has a keen appetite. ⟶	
● Mrs McBrien enjoys the company of others and is very sociable. ⟶	
● Mrs McBrien has good eyesight (when wearing spectacles) and quite good hearing. ⟶	
● Mrs McBrien likes to look her best and takes a great pride in her appearance. ⟶	
● Mrs McBrien reads well. ⟶	

6.4   Exercise: using strengths to develop a list of approaches for the client to reach his or her goal

Using the *strengths–needs list* that you have completed on the individual you are working with, review the Strengths to make a list of the ways that these can be used to help the client meet his or her GOAL. Refer to the example if you need assistance.

USING STRENGTHS TO DEVELOP A LIST OF APPROACHES FOR THE CLIENT TO REACH HIS OR HER GOAL

Name   **Date**

Goal decided upon for client

Strength (from Strengths–Needs list)	**Approaches** (Strengths can provide more than one approach)

SECTION 7

Breaking a goal down into smaller steps

7.1 So far we have completed the following stages of *goal planning*:

Completed the *Assessment Charts.*
Compiled an assessment of *strengths* and *needs.*
Selected a *need* to work on.
Written a *goal* to work towards.
Developed approaches for helping the client to meet the *goal* from the *strengths list.*

The next stage in making the *goal plan* is to consider how to break the *goal* down into smaller steps which can be achieved by the client fairly quickly.

7.2 How long the *goal* that you have selected for a client will take to achieve will depend on many things. These will include:

How quickly the client is able to learn new things
How far from achieving the *goal* the client is at the moment – what his or her present behaviour is in relation to the goal. (See section 5.1.)
What his or her attitude to *goal planning* in general seems to be and what he or she thinks about achieving the goal.

One of the most important things in *goal planning* is to ensure that the client quickly achieves success. If not, he or she may lose interest or become disheartened. Or *you* may become frustrated and disheartened.

On the other hand, successful achievement of the targets set will lead to increased confidence and interest.

7.3 For this reason, it is often necessary to break down the *goal* or *task* you have selected into a *series of smaller steps* which the client can achieve within a fairly short time.

It is difficult to make any hard and fast rules about how small or large the steps should be. As we said earlier, **(7.2)** this will depend on many things.

Two things are very important in breaking down the *goal* into steps:

(i) How much time you, or whoever is assisting the client with the *plan*, is able to spend with the client.

For example, you may only see the client once a week. Your client's goal may be going to the local shop. At present, s/he may only be able to go accompanied. S/he may need a lot of practice going to the shop accompanied by you, before moving on to going to the shop alone. It might be a good idea in this case to break the task down into many easier steps (say five or more steps). In this way the client might achieve each step in two sessions of practise (taking two weeks). If, on the other hand the steps were large (say you only had three steps or less), the client might need to practise each step four times. This would mean that each step would take a month to achieve. Example 7.4 shows the breaking down of such a *goal* into four steps. If you were only able to help Mrs McBrien, the lady in the example, once a week, it might be necessary to break the *goal* down into more steps. In this way Mrs McBrien could move on to the next step more quickly and this might boost her morale.

As a rule of thumb, try to break down the *goal* into smaller steps which the client can achieve *in a few days* – if you see the client often – or steps which can be achieved *in a couple of weeks* – if you only see the client about once a week.

(ii)   How many approaches you have been able to develop from the client's strengths list (Section 6).

Often the hardest task when writing a *goal plan* is getting started. We know what the client can do at the moment and we've been able to decide on a clear *goal* for the future, but how do we move the client on in the first step? By using one or more of the approaches that we've developed we can often get over this obstacle. It's easier still if we've a good range of approaches to choose from, and we can even combine two or more into one step.

For example, we may be worried that expecting a client who doesn't go out of the house to go to the nearest shop with someone may be asking too much and might lead to failure. However, we know that the client is an old friend of the local shopkeeper and is able to walk perfectly well around the house with a stick. Therefore, we can be fairly sure that these approaches can be built into a step that is not too large for the client. In this way we can use the information from the approaches to help us to make a start in writing the *goal plan*.

Since the approaches are based directly on the client's strengths, the help they give us in writing the steps of the *goal plan* is based firmly on the client's abilities. These steps should be written in the same clear, behavioural language as the *goal* (see Section 5).

7.4   Example of breaking a goal down into smaller steps

GOAL PLANNING SHEET

Client's name: Mrs McBrien   **Date:** 12.9.83

Present client behaviour: Mrs McBrien is physically able to dress herself but often gets the clothing in the wrong order. She also sometimes puts on inappropriate clothing.

Client's goal: Mrs McBrien will dress herself independently in indoor clothing, in the correct order every day.

GOAL PLAN:	Date achieved
1st step: Mrs McBrien will dress herself in suitable indoor clothing in the correct order when physically helped by a member of staff.	
2nd step: Mrs McBrien will dress herself in suitable indoor clothing in the correct order when verbally and gesturally prompted by a member of staff.	
3rd step: Mrs McBrien will dress herself in suitable indoor clothing in the correct order when given only three verbal reminders by a member of staff.	
4th step: Mrs McBrien will dress herself in suitable indoor clothing in the correct order when given only two verbal reminders by a member of staff.	
5th step: Mrs McBrien will dress herself in suitable in suitable indoor clothing in the correct order when reminded only once by a member of staff.	
6th step: Mrs McBrien will dress herself in suitable indoor clothing in the correct order when a member of staff observes her but doesn't give her any reminders.	
7th step: Mrs McBrien will dress herself in suitable indoor clothing in the correct order independently every day.	

7.5   Exercise: Look back to the approaches which could be used in Mr Hart's goal plan (6.2). Underline the approaches which we suggested in 6.2 and that we have used in the goal plan below

---

GOAL PLANNING SHEET

Client's name: Mr Hart   **Date:** 4.1.84

Present client behaviour: Mr Hart is able to walk well, but does not go out unless accompanied. He rarely sees people unless they call at the house.

Client's goal: Mr Hart will visit his friend in the next street twice a week. He will have a can of beer and/or read to his friend. He will do this independently.

GOAL PLAN:	Date achieved
1st step: Mr Hart will walk from his house to the local shop accompanied by a member of staff. He will go into the shop alone and buy a newspaper or some beer. He will walk to his friend's house accompanied, and read the newspaper to his friend and/or have a drink of beer. His friend will accompany him home.	
2nd step: Mr Hart will walk to the shop accompanied, and go into the shop and on to his friend's house alone. His friend will accompany him back as far as the local shop.	
3rd step: Mr Hart will walk to his friend's house via the corner shop alone. He will return home accompanied by his friend as far as the shop.	
4th step: Mr Hart will walk to and from his friend's house twice a week, unaccompanied.	

7.6 Exercise: Breaking down the goal into smaller steps. Try to use at least 4 steps

GOAL PLANNING SHEET

Client's name: Alfred Smith   **Date:** 21.9.83

Present client behaviour: Mr Smith has no physical handicaps. He will attempt to make a cup of tea when prompted, but makes a mess, does not let the water boil or the tea brew for long enough. He makes a sandwich when supervised and told what to do.

Client's goal: Mr Smith will make himself a cup of tea and a sandwich each afternoon without help or supervision.

GOAL PLAN: 1st step: 2nd step: 3rd step: 4th step:	Date achieved

7.7   Exercise: Using the approaches you developed from the strengths list and the goal you have selected, break down the goal for your client into at least 3 steps

GOAL PLANNING SHEET

Client's name:	**Date:**

Present client behaviour:

Client's goal:

GOAL PLAN:	**Date achieved**
1st step:	
2nd step:	
3rd step:	
4th step:	

SECTION 8

Recording the progress that your client makes

8.1 By now you will have been able to write a *goal plan* for your client. This will provide the basic structure for helping your client to meet his or her need. We have said that:

(a) the plan consists of a number of steps which form the path that the client takes to meet that need;

(b) each of these steps describes an aspect of the client's behaviour which can be gained in a week or two;

(c) the client *only* moves on from one step in the plan to the next when we are confident that his or her performance is competent.

8.2 In this section of the manual we want to introduce the way that we decide whether the client is 'successful' or not on the particular step that he or she is working on. The key to this involves recording the client's behaviour and using this objective and reliable information (remember Section 1?) to make your decision. By doing so we will make an accurate decision based on an objective assessment of the client's behaviour. If we relied solely on our memories and 'impressions' of how well a particular client had been doing the decision might easily be the wrong one.

8.3 A helpful way of recording this information (often called data) is the Goal Plan Progress Chart. A blank copy (**8.11**) is included in this section. Although it might at first seem a little complicated it will soon become a familiar form that is very easy to use.

8.4 The top right-hand corner contains the basic information you need to keep. It's important always to fill this in, especially the date at which you start using each chart – a different chart should be used for every week of skill training/goal planning. This way it will be possible to keep them in order for easy reference.

8.5 Immediately below that is a space for you to write the final *goal* that you are aiming at, and the current step that you are working on with the client. By writing these down clearly you will have a reminder of what you're hoping to achieve as well as how far you have got.

8.6 The lower part of the sheet is labelled 'Instructions'. This is where you describe *how* you carry out the step you are working on with your client. It must be written clearly so that anybody could use the instructions to carry out the *goal plan* and, furthermore, so that different people would all do so in the same way. The instructions should state how you record whether the client has been successful or not – according to the method you have described – and the number of occasions that the client works on the step each day/week. Keep your writing as brief as possible and use notes if you like. The example chart (**8.12**) will give you an idea of this.

8.7   As we have said, it is crucial to the *goal plan* that we know how well our client is doing on the step that s/he is working on. Use the box in the bottom half of the sheet to do this. Each time the client has a go at the particular steps s/he is currently working on, write down the date and put a ✓ or χ to indicate whether s/he has been successful or unsuccessful. If you have written your *goal plan* and instructions well, it should be very easy to decide whether a ✓ or χ is needed. You should not need to *interpret* the client's performance or give him/her the benefit of the doubt.

8.8   You can use this data to help you decide whether your client has successfully attained the step that he is working on. The best way of doing this is to measure the client's performance against a previously agreed target that you feel will be a good indicator of success. This is called the expected *criterion of success* and is written on the bottom line of the Goal Plan Progress Chart. This is the number of times that the client will successfully complete the step before moving on to the next. For instance, you will need to know that a client can do something, say four times out of five, before you know he or she is successful. To decide whether your client's performance on the step has been successful or not compare the data which you have recorded with that contained in the *criterion*. For example, if the data over a period of time showed that the client has successfully performed the step on four occasions out of five and the expected criteria of success has been 4/5 or 80% we would decide that the client has been successful. If instead the client had been correct on only three occasions out of five we would not say so.

8.9   This criterion must be arranged before you start working with your client on the step. By doing so, your decision will be more objective with less risk of your personal impressions interfering with your decision.

If we look at the top left hand of the sheet we can see that there are four outcomes for any step: (i) *successful* would refer to the case in which the client's performance equalled or exceeded the expected criterion. (ii) *continued* would usually refer to the situation where the client made good progress but had not achieved the expected criterion, but was expected to do so given time. (iii) *changed and continued* would be the outcome for a situation where the client had not reached the criterion, and it was also felt that he needed both more time and a slightly different method of achieving the step. (In this case the instructions would usually be modified, and sometimes the step itself. Discussion would be needed to clarify the situation.), (iv). Finally, an *abandoned* outcome refers to the situation where the client's progress was very poor indeed on the step and it was felt that the situation would not change significantly unless major alterations were made.

Therefore, on the basis of the data, you would place a ✓ on one of the *outcomes* in the top left hand corner. This then gives you an easy reference point for looking back over your work with the client. In the next section we will look at the best way of going about organising your *goal planning* and making the best decisions for your client.

8.10   Summary

It is very important to collect objective information about your client's performance on each step of the *goal-plan*. You need to know this in order to decide whether the client can move on to the next step towards the *goal*. The Goal Plan Progress Chart will help you to do this by telling you:

(a) Exactly how to help the client to complete the week's step in the *goal plan*, and how often he or she should attempt this.

(b) How to record success or failure on each attempt.

(c) How many times the client needs to be successful before you judge that he or she has achieved the step adequately.

(d) How to decide on the client's performance at the end of the week and plan for the following week.

8.11   Example of a blank Goal Plan Progress Chart

GOAL PLAN PROGRESS CHART

OUTCOME Successful	Name of client
Continued Changed and continued	Goal planner's name
Abandoned	Week beginning

Final goal

This week's step in GOAL PLAN

Instructions

No. of trial	1	2	3	4	5	6	7	8	9	10
Date										
Performance										
Expected criterion of success										

8.12   Example of a completed Goal Plan Progress Chart before use with client

GOAL PLAN PROGRESS CHART

OUTCOME Successful	Name of client: Mr Smart
Continued Changed and continued	Goal planner's name: Elsie
Abandoned	Week beginning: 10.5.83

Final goal: Mr Smart will walk from White Grove to the corner shop and back using his frame three times a week

This week's step in GOAL PLAN: Mr Smart will walk to the end of the main corridor and back once a day with verbal prompting by a member of staff.

Instructions:

1. Arrange the time for the exercise in advance with Mr Smart after having consulted the physiotherapist.
2. Clear other pieces of equipment and any obstacles from the main corridor.
3. Remind Mr Smart of how well he has done in the past and what the current step in his programme is.
4. Walk alongside Mr Smart offering encouragement every so often.
5. When Mr Smart reaches the end of the corridor congratulate him and after a brief rest encourage him to return to the beginning.
6. Meet Mr Smart at the other end and remind him how well he has done.
7. If Mr Smart achieves this place a ✓; if not place a ✗ on the chart.
8. Do this once a day

No. of trial	1	2	3	4	5	6	7	8	9	10
Date										
Performance										

Expected criterion of success: 6/7

8.13 Exercise in writing the instructions for a give step in a *goal plan*

GOAL PLAN PROGRESS CHART

OUTCOME	Name of client: Mrs Hicks
Successful	
Continued	**Goal planner's name:**
Changed and continued	
Abandoned	**Week beginning:** 10.5.83

Final goal: Mrs Hicks will independently shop for and correctly use diabetic foodstuffs at all meals.

This week's step in GOAL PLAN: Mrs Hicks will shop for diabetic foodstuffs independently and use them in her meals with a member of staff observing her but giving no guidance 3 times a week. (step 5 out of 7)

Instructions:

1. . . . .

2. . . . .

3. . . . .

4. . . . .

5. . . . .

6. . . . .

7. . . . .

No. of trial	1	2	3	4	5	6	7	8	9	10
Date										
Performance										

Expected criterion of success:

8.14 Exercise in writing a Goal Plan Progress Chart for your client

GOAL PLAN PROGRESS CHART

OUTCOME Successful	Name of client
Continued Changed and continued	Goal planner's name
Abandoned	Week beginning

Final goal

This week's step in GOAL PLAN

Instructions

No. of trial	1	2	3	4	5	6	7	8	9	10
Date										
Performance										

Expected criterion of success

8.15

GOAL PLAN PROGRESS CHART

OUTCOME Successful	Name of client
Continued Changed and continued	Goal planner's name
Abandoned	Week beginning

Final goal

This week's step in GOAL PLAN

Instructions

No. of trial	1	2	3	4	5	6	7	8	9	10
Date										
Performance										
Expected criterion of success										

SECTION 9

Writing the goal plan in clear behavioural language

9.1   This section is intended to remind you of the importance of writing each stage of the *goal plan* in *clear behavioural language*.

The final *goal* for the client, the *steps* towards the goal, and the *instructions* for carrying out the steps must all be written clearly.

9.2   Why clearly?

It is important that the *goal plan* be written clearly for the *client* so that he or she knows exactly what they are setting out to achieve, how much help they will receive in working towards it, and when they have reached the step or goal.

It is important for the *helpers* (staff, relatives, friends, etc.), so that everyone involved in the *goal plan* knows exactly what the client is aiming for, what they should do to help, and when it is achieved. In this way, everyone can help the client *in the same way* (be consistent) and everyone will know when the goal or step is achieved.

9.3   What is clear behavioural language?

Writing the *goal plan* in clear behavioural language means that you write the goals, steps and instructions in such a way that *two or more people reading the* goal plan *would agree exactly on the meaning and carry it out in exactly the same way.*

9.4   How plans go wrong if not written clearly

Perhaps you have identified a client, Mr Fielding, who has a need to have more company.

You write a *goal:* 'Mr Fielding will have more company', and a step towards the goal: 'Mr Fielding will get out more'.

The instructions for carrying out the plan you write are: 'Staff will encourage Mr Fielding to get out more'.

Because the *goal plan* is *not* written in clear behavioural language many problems will arise, for instance:

(i)   It will be impossible to know when the step or the goal has been achieved. What do 'have more company' and 'get out more' mean? It is likely that different people will disagree on this. If you and the client do not know what you are aiming for, how will you know when you have achieved it?

(ii)   It will be impossible for helpers to know how they should assist with the plan. What does 'encourage Mr Fielding to get out more' mean?: *Who* would do this? *What* would they do? *When* will they do it?

In Section 7 we have an example of a similar Goal for Mr Hart (see **7.5**). However, the *goal plan* for Mr Hart is written in *clear behavioural language*. Look back at this example.

9.5 Who? what? and when?

We have already practised writing goals and steps in clear behavioural language.
To be crystal clear, the goal and steps should say: *who* (the client's name) will be doing *what* and *when* they will be doing it.
   In the same way the instructions for carrying out the steps should specify:

   (*a*) *who* (person or persons) will be responsible for helping the client achieve each step;
   (*b*) *what* exactly they will be doing to help; and
   (*c*) *when* they will be doing it.

If the instructions are written clearly, it should be possible for anyone to pick up the *goal plan* and check that it is carried out in *exactly the same way* as anyone else.

SECTION 10
Goal planning in the future

10.1 By now you will have been able to draw up a *goal plan* for your individual client. As we have already discussed, the client should be able to attain the goal in quite a short period of time with each step taking a week or two. The information about the *goal plan* is contained on the Goal Planning Sheet (**7.7**) and you will have used the Goal Plan Progress Chart (**8.14**) to monitor and assess the progress of your client on each step of the *goal plan*. The data contained on the chart will enable you to decide whether your client has successfully achieved the particular step he/she was working on, according to the prearranged criteria of success you decided.

10.2 We have already discussed how the progress made by your client will be quite slow. Sometimes it is easier to start off a new way of working with clients than it is to keep it going. Slow progress, difficulties which aren't sorted out, staff changes and illnesses all combine sometimes to make it difficult to keep a new procedure going; it is often easier to return to the old, familiar routines.

In this section of the manual we wish to make a few suggestions about the way you can make it easier to keep going or maintain the goal planning procedures which you have put a great deal of effort into introducing to the establishment.

10.3 Although we have looked at how you make the decisions about your client's performance in the *goal plan,* it will help if you decide how to organise this. We recommend a weekly meeting at a *regular* time and place. This meeting should be brief but enable each client to be discussed, and his or her performance discussed. Decisions made at the meeting should be recorded in minutes which it is the Chairman's/Chairwoman's duty to take. This type of meeting has numerous advantages:

— Each client can be briefly discussed if necessary.
— Any difficulties or problems arising from the *goal plan* can be sorted out in the meeting and not left to build up or fall on one person's shoulders.
— The meeting and minutes recorded mean that everyone knows what decisions have been made. This will reduce any confusion or miscommunication.
— The meeting encourages staff to be *accountable* for their *goal plans* but *shares* the responsibility for the work. Little difficulties can best be sorted out if everyone can contribute before they become huge problems.
— A regular time and place for the meeting will encourage participation and increase the importance given to the meeting.

10.4   Example of the minutes of a weekly goal planning meeting

Present: Jack, Phyllis, Jenny, Linda, Paul, Carol.
Apologies: Joan (illness).

1. The minutes of the previous week's meeting were read and agreed.
2. *Mr Perkins*   Phyllis reported that he had done very well on this week's step, Step 4. He had been successful on all five trials and it was decided to try Step 5 – which involved reducing the amount of help being given to Mr Perkins on the same part of the task as Step 4 – next week.
3. *Mrs Harris*   Jenny reported that although her client had improved towards the end of the week, she had been successful on only 4 out of 8 trials. The criterion for success had been set at 6 out of 8, so it was decided to continue this step, Step 3, for another week.
4. *Mrs Bender*   Paul reported that he was having some difficulty in writing the *goal plan*. The meeting discussed this for a while and it was arranged that Carol should meet with Paul to help him with this during the next week.
5. *Mr Smith*   Paul reported he had started on Step 1 with Mr Smith's new *goal plan*. He had done very well and been successful on 7 out of 8 occasions. As the criterion was 70%, he was judged successful. Mr Smith will start on Step 2 over the next week.

Date and time of next meeting: 9.30 am, Tuesday 12th February.

SECTION 11
Building up the client's behaviours

11.1 Throughout this manual we have emphasised an approach to working with elderly clients which involves the development of programmes and plans to meet their needs. This has meant looking positively and optimistically at the client's abilities and structuring the way that these can be used to help meet the defined need. We hope the manual has helped you to develop the skills to do this.

11.2 However, even in centres for elderly people where the staff and helpers are using *goal planning* it is possible to find staff talking a lot about clients' 'behaviour problems'. It would be silly to pretend that difficulties do not exist, but we would like to spend a little time outlining an alternative way of looking at these 'problem' behaviours. The approach we will describe has many features in common with the *goal planning* that has been described in this Manual.

11.3 It is often easy to emphasise the difficulties or problems that a person has and to underestimate the possibilities that exist for change. We are all aware of this problem-oriented approach. To replace this we prefer a different way of considering problems or difficulties, often called the *constructional* approach. This looks at a person's difficulties in terms of *behaviours* and analyses them together with the other important events in the situation. Most important, it understands that these behaviours *are able to change,* that there are many aspects of these behaviours that are of value to the individual, and that these can be used to encourage the development of ways of behaving which are of more use to the client. This approach gets its name because it encourages the 'construction' of more acceptable/valuable behaviours that do not cause problems for the client or others. The other approach – sometimes called 'pathological' – in contrast, involves only reducing or removing behaviours that it describes as 'problems'.

11.4 The main features of the 'constructional' and 'pathological' approaches

Constructional approach	Pathological approach
Accepts difficulties but analyses the behaviours involved	Emphasises 'problems'
Builds up person's behaviour	Reduces/eliminates person's problem behaviour(s)
Increases person's range of behaviours	Often – but not necessarily always – reduces person's range of behaviours

11.5   We feel strongly that in many situations the reduction of a person's behaviour is not helpful to that person and is possibly unethical. One reason for this is that if there are only a limited range of opportunities – and therefore behaviours – available to a person we should not be looking at ways of reducing these further. Instead, we should be attempting to expand the individual's range of opportunities and abilities. Another reason for using a constructional approach concerns practicality. If a person has only a limited range of behaviours it is often very difficult actually to reduce them further. This may be because these behaviours enable the individual to obtain some rewards from the environment which he or she would not otherwise get.

11.6   We have said that the constructional approach involves *increasing* the options available to the person rather than reducing them. It involves looking clearly at the individual's behaviour and how this interacts with other factors in the environment. It is quite easy – if we are determined – to stop or reduce a particular behaviour, e.g. chemical or physical restraints can 'stop' wandering or reduce 'chattering'. It is not so easy to develop patterns of more appropriate behaviour which are satisfying to the client. To illustrate the difference between this and the, more common, problem-orientated approach we will look at the key points in the constructional approach.

Before this, there is an exercise (**11.11**) which will help you to consider the more obvious differences between the two approaches.

11.7   The constructional approach does not ignore problems or difficulties caused by a person's behaviour. Its purpose is to help these, but to do so by developing new ways for the client to behave. For this to happen we need to state very clearly the outcome of any work with the client – just as we needed to state clearly the goal in our *goal planning*. In this way we can see that although the outcomes of these two approaches are similar in the sense that they both reduce distress to the client or staff, they are really very different when one considers the changes they have on the client's behaviours.

e.g. Mr Cleary mumbles and doesn't make much sense.

Pathological/problem-oriented approach: prescribe tranquilising medicine or ignore Mr Cleary's attempts to use language.

Constructional approach: progressively improve the quality of Mr Cleary's speech and increase the proportion of it which makes sense to other elderly clients.

11.8   Another distinctive quality of this approach is the way that it uses the client's current level of behaviour as a *starting point* for behaviour change. This, of course, follows on directly from the idea of building behaviour up, but emphasises also the way in which 'problem' behaviours can be developed and used to reach a more appropriate objective. This is closely connected with our analysis of how the 'problem' behaviour 'works' for the client in his or her environment (refer to **11.5**).

11.9   The constructional approach to so-called problems therefore involves us changing our attitudes about the way we work with clients. In particular we can see that this work is much more effective and appropriate for the client if:

   (*a*) we concentrate on the behaviours which we wish to establish and develop rather than on those to be eliminated or reduced;
   (b) we look at behaviours positively rather than negatively;
   (*c*) we consider a person's strengths rather than their weaknesses.

Furthermore, the constructional approach requires us to consider the problem in terms of wider aspects of the client's behaviour and other things going on in the environment. Instead of interpreting the difficult behaviour as part of a *problem* in its own right, we should recognise that the pattern of behaviour may be appropriate, sensible and effective for the client given the satisfactions that are available in the environment at a particular time. Behaviour which may be inaccurately described as 'confused', 'bloody-minded' or 'stupid' may actually be exactly tailored to achieve the rewards which are available.

11.10 It can be seen that *goal planning* fits into this approach of working with clients. Through the process of assessing a person's strengths and needs and forming goal plans to help construct behaviours for the client we are employing the main points of the constructional approach. The emphasis is firmly placed on extending the behaviours available to the client, and we hope that as you become more experienced in goal planning with your clients you may be able to use wider aspects of the constructional approach in your work with elderly individuals.

11.11 Exercise in developing constructional approaches to dealing with some common 'problem behaviours'

Look at the examples below. They are brief descriptions of a person's behaviour which is causing 'problems', and the way that people involved with the client decided to approach the situation. Place a tick (✔) by the side of the approaches that you consider to be 'constructional' and a cross (✗) by the side of those that are more 'pathological'.

1. After a lifetime of living alone in a small village on the edge of town, Miss Clark has had to be admitted to an elderly persons' home. Soon after her admission to an upstairs wing she began to wander and has been prescribed a tranquilliser to soothe her and help prevent the wandering. ☐

2. An analysis of Mrs Pike's 'shouting' suggested that it occurred before she needed to be assisted to the toilet. The staff in the day centre had originally considered asking the visiting psychogeriatrician to assess Mrs Pike, but have now begun to teach her another way of letting people know of her physical needs. ☐

3. Mr Stolz is a sprightly and aware man aged 76. He lives in a small old people's home and is described by the staff as the 'life and soul of most of the parties' there. He has suddenly started to become incontinent on an occasional basis during day and night. A meeting of the staff decided to regularly toilet Mr Stolz as a matter of course to 'prevent' his incontinence. ☐

4. Mr Case had been a very active man in his earlier working life. Now aged 72, but physically quite able, he attends the day centre three days each week. Neighbours and staff had voiced their worries about Mr Case's wandering. After completing an assessment of his abilities and needs, and having discussed the issue with him, staff decided to start a programme which aimed to encourage Mr Case to make short, purposeful walks in his locality to meet old friends and socialise. ☐

5. Although physically and intellectually very fit, Mrs James was referred to the day centre by her G.P. for 'socialisation' and 'day care'. No specific plans were made for helping Mrs James to meet any of her needs. ☐

6. Mr Talbot's 'fussing' had earlier been treated as 'just his way of doing things'

by staff and residents of the EPH home he lived in. However, it had now become a real problem and he had been found hoarding crockery and items of clothing. It had been suggested that he should be restricted to certain areas of the home and closely watched, and even that the doctor's advice should be sought. Instead, after a long discussion about Mr Talbot's behaviour and his needs it was decided to try encouraging him to take an active part in domestic duties inside the home, including monitoring the laundry each week.

APPENDIX 1
Elderly Person's Assessment Charts

1.1   Elderly Person's Assessment Chart

ELDERLY PERSON'S ASSESSMENT CHART
Client's name
Age
Date of birth
Address
Assessor's name
Name of relatives etc. assisting with Assessment
Date completed

ASSESSMENT   Section 1

Please tick the most appropriate answer

SENSORY ABILITIES

| **Dentures** | Has own teeth |
| | Has dentures |

Eyesight	Can see (or can see with glasses)
	Partially blind
	Totally blind

Hearing	No hearing difficulties without hearing aid
	No hearing difficulties, though requires hearing aid
	Has hearing difficulties which interfere with communication

MOBILITY

Walking	No difficulty in walking
	Walks unsteadily without aid or uses stick
	Walks only with aid (frame, tripod) or physical assistance
	Unable to walk and chairbound/bedfast

Stairs	Able to go up and down stairs independently
	Able to go up and down stairs with physical assistance or handrail
	Unable to go up and down stairs

Ability to go out of house	Able to use public transport independently
	Able to shop locally, visit neighbours etc. independently
	Unable to leave house unless accompanied
Frequency of leaving house	Gets out of house regularly (at least once a week)
	Gets out of house infrequently (at least once a month)
	Never or rarely gets out of house (less than once a month)

SOCIAL CONTACTS

Visits others, or has visitors regularly (every day)

Visits others or has visitors (at least once a week)

Visits others or has visitors rarely (once a month or less)

Please specify regular social contacts:

ASSESSMENT   Section 2(a)

Please tick the most appropriate column

PERSONAL SELF-HELP SKILLS

	Can do without help or supervision	Can do with minimum help or supervision	Requires maximum help or supervision	No opportunity to find out or observe
1 Undressing/dressing				
Completely dresses self, including difficult fastenings (e.g. zips, buttons)				
Completely undresses self, including difficult fastenings				
Dresses self in sensible sequence (e.g. does not put shoes on before socks)				
2 Selection of clothing				
Selects own clothes from drawer or wardrobe				
Chooses clothing and footwear appropriate to occasion (e.g. bed, shopping and weather conditions)				
3 Use of Toilet				
* Toilets self (daytime)				
* Toilets self (night-time)				
Wipes self, flushes toilet and adjusts clothing				
4 Personal Hygiene				
Washes hands and face when needed (e.g. in morning, after toilet, etc.)				
Has bath or shower when needed				
Attends to oral hygiene				
Washes hair				
Combs or brushes hair				
Shaves				
Changes underwear and socks/stockings/tights regularly				
5 Eating				
Uses knife, fork and spoon appropriately				
Table habits acceptable (e.g. no spilling, eats at a correct speed, etc.)				

* If incontinent, specify whether of urine or faeces or both

Specify frequency

ASSESSMENT   Section 2(b)

Please tick the most appropriate column

	Can do without help or supervision	Can do with minimum help or supervision	Requires maximum help or supervision	No opportunity to find out or observe
DOMESTIC SELF-HELP SKILLS				
Washes clothes by hand				
Washes clothes (by machine)				
Irons				
Makes hot drinks				
Makes simple snacks				
Makes cooked meals				
Sets and clears table				
Washes, dries and puts items away				
Makes bed				
Dusts				
Vacuums				
Cleans Windows				
SHOPPING AND HANDLING MONEY				
Shops for food and household needs				
Shops for other personal needs				
Pays bills, rent, collects pension				
Competent in handling money (can add coins together to pay and can check change)				
COMMUNICATION				
Understands what others say				
Is able to make self understood by others				
Writes letters or messages				
Uses telephone				
OCCUPATION				
Keeps self occupied with purposeful activities				
FIRST AID AND HEALTH				
Seeks medical help when required				
Takes medicines reliably				
Shows awareness of danger and exercises caution				
ORIENTATION AND MEMORY				
Knows full name, age, date of birth				
Knows approximate time, knows month, year				
Knows address				
Finds way about house				
Finds way about neighbourhood				
Recognises familiar people				
Can remember simple instructions				

APPENDIX II
Completing the Assessment Charts

11.1 Completing Section 1

This section covers *sensory abilities* (eyesight, hearing); *mobility*; and *social contact*.

(i) *Sensory abilities*

It is very important that we find out if an elderly person can see and hear adequately. This may sound obvious. However, if a person has difficulty with their sight or hearing it may affect their ability to do many things and consequently result in other problems developing.

For example, if someone has difficulty in seeing, they may have a problem finding their bearings when they go to a new place. If, additionally, they are upset or anxious, as they might be in new circumstances, such as going into hospital or attending a day centre for the first time, then this will add to their problem fo learning their way about.

Very often a person who is old and has difficulty in finding his or her way around is described as 'confused' or 'disoriented' or, worse still, possibly 'dementing'. In this example part of his/her confusion and disorientation could be remedied by making sure that s/he can see adequately.

Similarly, uncorrected hearing problems can affect many aspects of behaviour. This can be demonstrated by a simple experiment. If you plug your ears then try to have a conversation with someone you will begin to appreciate how hearing difficulties may affect the way you get along with other people. It's likely that after a while you'll begin to get frustrated with trying to understand what the other person is saying. Perhaps you'll feel irritated, or just bored and will want to bring the conversation to a close.

A person who is elderly, and who becomes irritable with others or doesn't seem interested in talking is often described as 'socially withdrawn' or 'bad tempered'. In this example, his or her mood and social withdrawal might be remedied by ensuring that hearing problems are corrected.

The 'Sensory abilities' part of Section 1 is relatively straightforward to complete.

(a) Check whether the person has a hearing aid and/or spectacles. S/he may well have such aids but for some reason does not use them: perhaps they need replacing, or perhaps they're lost, or for some other reason the person may prefer not to use them. It may be necessary to check this information with a relative.

(b) If the person has a hearing aid or spectacles, encourage him/her to use them while you are making your observations and assessments.

(c) *Sight*: Observations to assess whether a person has difficulties might include:
Can the person recognise a familiar person across the room?
Can the person count fingers at one yard?
Can the person read the headline of a paper?

Can the person read normal text?

If a person cannot, there may be other reasons why this is so, other than poor eyesight. For example, s/he may be unable to read or may have difficulty in recognising people due to some physical problem, perhaps due to a stroke. However, if you have any doubts about a person's sight, it is best to encourage him/her to get his eyes tested or to organise this.

(d) *Hearing*: Observations to assess whether a person has difficulties might include:

Can the person hear normal conversation when looking towards?

Can the person hear normal conversation when looking away?

Can the person hear loud conversation when looking towards?

Can the person hear loud conversation when looking away?

Again, if a person has problems with these observations, it may not be because s/he is hard of hearing. S/he may *hear* the words but not *understand* them.

This sometimes happens when a person has had a stroke, and the problems need to be looked at more closely in the 'Communication' part of Section 2 of the charts. However, if you have any doubts about a person's hearing it is best to try and arrange for it to be tested.

(ii)   *Mobility and social contact*

The first two parts of the mobility items may be completed from your observations (walking, stairs). If there are no stairs in the setting in which you work, it may be necessary to observe the elderly person in a different setting (e.g. at home) in order to complete this assessment.

A person's 'ability to go out of the house' may be assessed by asking the person and also other people who are in close contact with him/her. Similarly with 'frequency of leaving the house'.

It is important to specify who the regular social contacts are, because these people may be useful in assisting in any plans that you draw up to help the elderly client.

11.2 Assessment of sight and hearing task

Select a person who attends your unit. Complete the sight and hearing assessments.

Client's name

Sight	**Hearing**
Does	Does ....
wear spectacles?	have a hearing aid?
Recognise familiar person?	Hear normal conversation looking towards?
Count fingers at one yard?	Hear normal conversation looking away?
Read headline of a paper?	Hear loud conversation looking towards?
Read normal text?	Hear loud conversation looking away?
Comments	*Comments*
....	....
....	....
....	....

11.3 Completing Section 2

This section covers *personal self-help skills* (things like dressing and washing), *domestic self-help skills* (things like housework and cooking), *shopping and handling money, communication, occupation, first aid and health* and *orientation and memory*.

   For each item of behaviour listed in section 2 of the charts you are required to tick one of 4 boxes.

For example:	Can do without help or supervision	Can do with minimum help or supervision	Requires maximum help or supervision	No opportunity to find out or observe
Completely undresses self, including difficult fastenings (e.g. zips, buttons)				

How do you decide which box to tick?

(i) *Collecting information*
For many of the items in Section 2 you may have no opportunity to observe *for yourself*. This will be likely if you only see the client *during the day* and do not see him/her *in their home*.

   There are several ways to collect the information, even when you have not observed the behaviour.

(*a*) Ask the client about all of the items in Section 2 of the charts. It may be that the information you get from the client is not completely *reliable*. This can happen for several reasons and it will mean that you should also try to ask others who know the client well or, better still, observe the client's actual behaviour yourself.

(*b*) *Ask someone who knows the client well.* This is important, but may not give you *reliable* information because of the reasons above. Be cautious, therefore, of the information you get. If in doubt, try to observe the client. You may be 'in doubt' if: *the person's information is different to what the client says,* or if *the person's information is different to the things you have seen the client do.* This is not to say that the client or the person you ask is not telling the truth – just that it is difficult to stand back and be objective about our own behaviour or that of people we know well.

(*c*) *Observe the client.* This is the best method of assessment. Try to observe the client performing the task you are uncertain about assessing. *If you do not have the opportunity to* **observe** *the client performing any item in the charts* **and** *you are unsure about the* **reliability** *of what the client and other people say, tick the box 'no opportunity to observe or find out'.* It would not be sensible to collect information which is wrong or inaccurate. It could lead to plans for the client which you base on this information going wrong.

(ii) *Filling in the boxes*
If after collecting information on an item in Section 2 you feel able to make an assessment then you need to decide which of the boxes you should tick. These are shown in the example.

   Can do without help or supervision. To tick this box the client should be able *to do the task without any help at all. He or she should not need anyone there to help or encourage* him/her.

   Can do with minimum help or supervision. To tick this box the client *should be able to do the task with very little help.* This means *s/he needs only two or three bits of physical guidance.* Or s/he may need *someone standing by to give spoken help or encouragement.*

   Requires maximum help or supervision. If the client needs *more help than that stated above* (two or three bits of physical help and or spoken help or encouragement) then tick this box.

The important rule in completing Section 2 of the Charts is: **If you are in doubt which box to tick: observe the client for yourself** *or* **tick 'no opportunity to observe or find out'. Try and observe when you have time if this information is important to the client's plan.**

A complete example of a goal plan

This example starts with basic assessment information about Mr Jones. It shows how this information is used to complete all the stages we have presented in this manual. At the end a completed *goal plan* and the progress made by Mr Jones on a particular step are shown.

III.1 Client assessment information

Mr Jones is a 69-year-old widower who lives alone in a warden-controlled flat. He was referred to the day centre when he came out of hospital following a fall whilst shopping at the local shops. He now walks unsteadily and dislikes walking outside alone. This irritates him because he values his independence.

His wife died two years earlier and he moved from their house to the flat because he felt he needed a change, and also because he was nervous at night on his own. The flat is in a different area, and he knows very few people who live in the flats or thereabouts. He is on friendly terms with two gentlemen in the flats. He has a home-help with whom he gets on well. He can cook snacks, but never learned to cook meals. In terms of self care, he is fully independent apart from cooking, shopping and jobs involving reaching, e.g. cleaning windows.

Mr Jones attends the day centre on two days a week where he mixes well, but does little to occupy himself. At home, he only goes out when his son takes him in the car (about once a month). He spends some of his time reading, doing bits of housework, or just looking out of the window.

He used to enjoy sports and until his wife died he played bowls at the local park. He and his wife used to enjoy a sociable drink at the British Legion Club across the road from their house several times a week.

Staff have discussed *goal planning* with Mr Jones and he says he is keen to be involved.

III.2 Strengths–needs list

STRENGTHS–NEEDS LIST

Client: Mr Jones   **Date:** 27.7.83

Strengths	Needs
What the individual can do, what s/he likes to do, and other people who are willing to help	State these positively – what s/he should be doing

Strengths

What the individual can do, what s/he likes to do, and other people who are willing to help

- Mr Jones can walk, though unsteadily.
- Mr Jones has shopping skills.
- Mr Jones has 2 friends locally.
- Mr Jones has many independent self-help skills.
- Mr Jones is willing to be involved in *goal planning*.
- Mr Jones is generally fit and able apart from reaching and his unsteady gait.
- Mr Jones has no sensory handicaps.
- Mr Jones socialises well.
- Mr Jones' son comes to visit once a month and they get on quite well.
- Mr Jones likes to read.
- Mr Jones enjoys sports.
- Mr Jones used to enjoy bowls.
- Mr Jones used to enjoy a drink.
- Mr Jones can cook snacks.
- Mr Jones gets on well with his home-help.

Needs

State these positively – what s/he should be doing

- Mr Jones needs to be able to walk more steadily.
- Mr Jones needs to make more friends/acquaintances.
- Mr Jones needs to be able to cook meals.
- Mr Jones needs to be able to go shopping.
- Mr Jones needs to be able to go out alone without being afraid of falling.
- Mr Jones needs to develop more interests at home and occupation at the day centre.

III.3   Exercise in selecting a need from the strengths–needs list

1. Look back to the *strengths–needs list* which you completed in the last session.
2. Select *one* need from the list to work with, using the guidelines just discussed.
3. Give the reasons why you selected the need in the space below:

SELECTING A NEED FROM THE STRENGTHS–NEEDS LIST
Name of client: Mr Jones
Need selected to work on: Mr Jones needs to be able to go out alone without being afraid of falling.
Reasons for selecting the need (1) Staff feel that the goal will be successfully accomplished quite quickly. (2) In discussion, Mr Jones has said that he is keen to overcome his fears and regain his independence. (3) Important to Mr Jones since it makes it easier to work on his other needs (e.g. going shopping, making friends).

III.4 Stating chosen need as a clear goal

STATING CHOSEN NEED AS A CLEAR GOAL
Name of client: Mr Jones
Need selected to work on: Mr Jones needs to be able to go out alone without being afraid of falling.
Clear GOAL for your client to meet: Mr Jones will go to the local Spar shop (450 yards away from his home) and then meet one of his friends 'from the flats' in the British Legion – almost next door to the shop – for a drink. He will do this twice a week at lunchtime.

III.5   Exercise: using strengths to develop a list of approaches for the client to reach his or her goal

Using the strengths–needs list that you have completed on the individual you are working with, review the strengths to make a list of the ways that these can be used to help the client meet his or her goal. Refer to the example if you need assistance.

USING STRENGTHS TO DEVELOP A LIST OF APPROACHES FOR THE CLIENT TO REACH HIS OR HER GOAL

Name: Mr Jones   **Date:** 2/8/83

Goal decided upon for client: Mr Jones will go to the local Spar shop and then meet one of his friends from the flats for a drink in the British Legion. He will do this twice a week at lunchtimes.

Strength (from Strengths–Needs list)	Approaches (Strengths can provide more than one approach)
Mr Jones can walk, although unsteadily.	This will obviously help in the *goal plan*. We can build on these already existing skills.
Mr Jones socialises well and has two friends in the WC flats where he lives.	This will help Mr Jones in getting out and meeting people, including the shopkeeper – a local woman. Meeting his friend for a drink will be a natural thing to do.
Mr Jones used to like going out for a drink.	Having a drink after the visit to the shop is both rewarding for Mr Jones and quite a natural thing to do in his experience. It may encourage him to do the journey.
Mr Jones has shopping skills.	This will make going to the shop easier and less frightening for Mr Jones. He will feel a sense of achievement in being able to buy things for himself.
Mr Jones has no sensory handicaps.	This will help Mr Jones to recognise where he's going, to do his shopping and to converse with people on the way.
Mr Jones is willing to be involved in the *goal plan*.	We can use this fact to encourage Mr Jones at each step of the plan and discuss progress and any difficulties which may be arising, etc.

III.6   Goal planning sheet

GOAL PLANNING SHEET

Client's name: Mr Jones   **Date:** 10.8.83

Present client behaviour: Mr Jones can walk unsteadily and is very sociable but is afraid of going out walking since a fall.

Client's goal: Mr Jones will go unaccompanied to the local Spar shop and then meet one of his friends from the flats in the British Legion. He will do this at lunchtimes, twice a week.

GOAL PLAN:	Date achieved
1st step: Mr Jones will go to the Spar shop accompanied by his helper, Sarah, and then return home.	
2nd step: Mr Jones will go to the Spar shop accompanied by his helper, Sarah, and return home on his own with a little shopping, to be met there by Sarah.	
3rd step: Mr Jones will meet his helper, Sarah, half way to the Spar shop. She will then accompany him the rest of the way. After buying his shopping Mr Jones will return home, unaccompanied, to be met there by Sarah.	
4th step: Mr Jones will walk unaccompanied to the Spar shop and meet Sarah there. After doing his shopping she will accompany him to the club next door. He will meet his pal there and have a drink. They will return home together.	
5th step: Mr Jones will go to the Spar shop unaccompanied and do a little shopping. He will then go unaccompanied to the British Legion and meet Sarah and his friend there. After a drink he will go home with his friend.	
6th step: Mr Jones will go unaccompanied to the Spar shop and get some shopping. Afterwards, he will go unaccompanied to the British Legion and meet his friend there for a drink. Afterwards he will make his way home. Sarah will pop around later to see if everything went well.	
7th step: Mr Jones will go unaccompanied to the Spar shop and get some shopping. Afterwards, he will go unaccompanied to the British Legion and meet his friend there for a drink. Afterwards he will make his way home.	

III.7   Goal Plan Progress Chart

GOAL PLAN PROGRESS CHART

OUTCOME Successful ✓	Name of client: Mr Jones
Continued Changed and continued	Goal planner's name: Sarah
Abandoned	Week beginning: 6.10.83

Final goal: Mr Jones will go unaccompanied to the Spar shop and then meet one of his friends from the flats in the British Legion. He will do this at lunchtimes, twice a week

This week's step in GOAL PLAN: Mr Jones will meet Sarah half-way to the Spar shop. She will accompany him to the shop, and after buying his shopping Mr Jones will return home unaccompanied

Instructions:

1. Meet Mr Jones at the corner of Ethel Road (half-way between his house and the shop) at a pre-arranged time.
2. Congratulate Mr Jones on his achievement and accompany him to the shop.
3. Talk with Mr Jones and the shopkeeper while he does his shopping. Remind him of how well he is doing and what he'll have for his tea that day.
4. When Mr Jones has finished in the shop, arrange to meet him back at home and make an excuse to leave.
5. From a distance watch Mr Jones make his way back home alone.
6. Call round to the home and tell Mr Jones how pleased you are with his progress. If he achieved this, place a ✓ blow. If not, place a χ.
7. Do this twice a week at pre-arranged times.

No. of trial	1	2	3	4	5	6	7	8	9	10
Date	8.10.83	11.10.83	15.10.83	17.10.83						
Performance	✓	χ	✓	✓						
Expected criterion of success: 3/4										

Instructors' guidelines for setting up, conducting and evaluating a goal planning workshop

Introduction

The manual is designed for use under the guidance of someone who is already familiar with the techniques of *goal planning*. In this appendix we shall refer to such a person as an 'instructor', and to those staff or others who are learning the techniques as 'trainees'. The purpose of the appendix is to provide guidelines on the instructor's role in the training. We also include advice on who to train, how to evaluate the training, and how best to maintain the *goal planning* after training.

The authors have always worked through the content of the manual with a group of trainees, rather than used individual teaching. The former workshop format offers a number of advantages in terms of economy of time, group support in carrying out plans and so on. The guidelines in this appendix are specifically directed to running a Goal Planning Workshop. However, it is quite possible to instruct an individual in how to carry out *goal plans*. The guidelines contained herein should also be of relevance to such individual guidance.

We should emphasise that the manual aims to assist in teaching trainees *goal planning* skills through *practice*. Practising the components of *goal planning* by working with a client is an *essential* part of the training. The instructor needs to take this into account when planning training sessions: it is essential to allow time for the trainees to practise their skills with clients between sessions.

1. Setting up a Goal Planning Workshop

(i) *What experience does the instructor need*? It is difficult to make hard and fast rules about who will be successful in running a Goal Planning Workshop. In the final analysis the evaluation exercises (see p. 76 and the monitoring of the outcome of the *goal plans* at goal planning meetings (see Section 10) will assist you in assessing the success of the training.

The training format is geared to the trainees acquiring practical experience. Consequently it makes sense that you should have acquired sufficient practical experience in *goal planning* yourself prior to guiding others in the techniques. We would strongly recommend that you acquire the following knowledge and practical experience before embarking on running a Workshop.

(*a*) You should be very familiar with the information in the manual. This includes having worked through the examples and exercises for yourself.
(*b*) You should have formulated and carried out *goal plans* with *at least six* elderly clients. We feel that this is the minimum practical experience you need to have acquired in order to begin to share your skills with others.

(ii) *What preparation is required before beginning a workshop*? The training programme is designed for people who have a long term and regular contact with elderly clients. This is a prerequisite for them to be able to carry out plans over a period of weeks or months. The staff selected for training must also have the opportunity to carry out goal plans after training. This will require their attendance at weekly meetings (see Section 10) in order to review the plans and also will necessitate the availability of continued support and supervision in their work. These issues of *generalisation* and *maintenance*** need to be taken into consideration before you commence instruction.

Our experience of tackling these issues suggests that you should try and adhere to the following guidelines:

(*a*) Select trainees from an establishment or work setting where staff and their managers are willing and keen to try out new ideas. We know that the approach of *goal planning* will not be maintained after training unless the organisation in which the staff work actively supports and seeks to maintain the new method of working. It is extremely difficult to change organisations (unless you happen to be the head of one!). Consequently, it makes sense to try out *goal planning* with elderly clients in an organisation which *is* relatively sympathetic to the approach at the outset.

(*b*) Following the training, the weekly *goal planning* meetings and the availability of further help and support will be necessary for the trainees. It may be that you will be able to attend the weekly meetings and provide the continued support indefinitely. However, in some cases you may be able to offer involvement only for a limited time period. In such cases it is important to identify an individual in the work setting who will continue the role of maintaining the *goal planning*. For convenience sake we might call this person the 'manager', and it may be useful if they do have a general managerial role in the organisation. It is important that the instructor attends the Goal Planning meeting for several months after training to assist in consolidating the skills required. This time might be used to 'coach' the manager in the skills required to take over your role at a specified date.

(*c*) It will be necessary for you to obtain the following commitments from the organisation prior to commencing the training:

Time-off from other duties to allow staff to attend the workshop (see timetable). Similarly, time for staff to attend the weekly meetings following training, and also to formulate and carry out the Goal Plans as part of their work duties.
Time for the 'manager' to carry out the supervision and support work; also secretarial support for typing and duplicating the weekly Goal Planning Minutes, etc.
If it is felt necessary, an undertaking that any increased 'risks' the *goal plans* may involve for the clients will be accepted by the organisation as a whole.
All this may sound very formal. However, our experience suggests that dealing with these issues before training can save a lot of problems later on!

Furthermore, we would recommend that you obtain a written commitment regarding the above points whenever possible.

* For those unfamiliar with the literature concerning these issues, useful papers to read are:
Georgiades, N. J. and Phillimore, L. (1975). 'The myth of the hero-innovator and alternative strategies for organisational change'. *In* Kiernan, C. and Woodford, P. F. (eds.) *Behaviour Modification with the Severely Retarded*. Amsterdam, Associated Scientific Publishers.
Ivancic, M. T., Reid, D. H., Iwata, B. A., Faw, G. D. and Page, T. J. (1981). 'Evaluating a supervision programme for developing and maintaining therapeutic staff-resident interactions during institutional care routines'. *Journal of Applied Behaviour Analysis,* 14, 95–107.
Sanders, M. R. and James, J. E. (1983). 'The modification of behaviour. A review of generalisation and maintenance'. *Behaviour Modification,* 7, 3–27.

(iii) *How many trainees should be included in a workshop? How long does the training take?* In considering how many trainees to have on the workshop, the chief consideration is adequate individual supervision and feedback from the practical exercises. We would recommend that no more than ten trainees are included in a workshop which has two instructors.

The authors have used two time schedules for the workshops: weekly sessions lasting approximately one hour and extending over a period of months; and 'block' training over two and a half days. We would strongly recommend the latter, or if that is impracticable then some variation, for example, six half days.

If the training extends over a relatively long time period (say, beyond a month), then there may be many delays. Staff absences, holidays, etc. may necessitate going over material for those who were unable to attend the previous session. These delays can interrupt the momentum of the training.

Whatever format for scheduling the training is selected, *it is essential* that you allow sufficient breaks between sessions to permit the trainees to try out work covered in the training with elderly clients.

Included below is a recommended timetable for a Goal Planning Workshop. Obviously, it may be necessary to modify the times according to your specific needs and the constraints of your work setting.

GOAL PLANNING WORKSHOP

Recommended timetable
(See Instructors' Notes concerning alternatives to using video)

Day 1		*Time*
9.30 am	Coffee and Introductions	
9.45	*Assessment and Observations* (Section 1)	20 mins
	Introduction and example	
	*Video tape exercise	25 mins
10.30	*The Assessment Charts* (Section 2)	
	Introduction to Charts	30 mins
11.00	*Video of client interview	
	*Video of relative interview	
	Discussion of video tapes and points arising	1 hour
12.00	*Strengths and Needs List* (Section 3)	
	Introduction and Examples	30 mins
	Group Exercises and feedback	30 mins
1.00 pm	finish	

'Homework' assignment for Day 2:
Assess an elderly client using the Charts
Perform exercise 1.9 if not already completed
Draw up *strengths–needs List*

Allow approximately one week between Day 1 and Day 2

Day 2

9.15 am	Small group discussion of 'homework'	
	Feedback on assessment and *strengths–needs list*	1¼ hours

10.30	Coffee	
10.45	*Selecting a need and writing as a clear goal* (Sections 4 and 5)	
	Introduction and examples	30 mins
	Group exercise and feedback	30 mins
11.45	*Developing Approaches from strengths–needs list* (Section 6)	
	Introduction and examples	30 mins
	Group exercise and feedback	30 mins
12.45	Lunch	
1.45 pm	*The Goal Plan* (Section 7)	
	Introduction; breaking goals into steps and examples	30 mins
	Group exercises – drawing up a *practice goal plan*	45 mins
3.00	Feedback from small groups	60 mins
4.00	Finish	
	'Homework' assignment for Day 3:	
	Write *goal plan* for individual clients	

Day 3

9.15 am	Summary of training covered	75 mins
	Feedback from writing *goal plans*	
10.30	*Goal Plan Progress Chart* (Section 8)	
	Introduction and examples	30 mins
	Group exercises	30 mins
	Group feedback	30 mins
12.00	*Using clear behavioural language* (Section 9)	
	Introduction; examples and exercises	30 mins
12.30 pm	Lunch	
1.30	*Goal Planning Meetings* (Section 10)	
	Introduction	
	*Video and discussion	45 mins
2.15	*Constructional approach* (Section 11)	
	Introduction; example and exercises	30 mins
	Coffee	
2.45	*Completed example of Goal Plan*	15 mins
3.00	Feedback and discussion	
3.15	Evaluation exercises	

(iv)   *What additional equipment is required for running the course?*

*Use of video film
We have suggested that video films may be useful adjuncts to the workshop in presenting the material and carrying out the exercises in Sections 1 and 10. (See Instructors' Notes for the relevant sections.)

However, we should stress that such use of filmed behaviour is *not* a prerequisite to conducting the workshop. Alternative means of presenting the material and carrying out the exercises are given in the Instructors' Notes.

Use of overhead projector

The authors have found the overhead projector a useful teaching aid in two ways:

1. To display the main points from sections of the manual.
2. By asking the trainees to put the results of their group work and homework (see Instructors' Notes) on acetates so the whole group can benefit from the instructors' feedback.

2. Conducting a Goal Planning Workshop

(i) *Some general points about the instructor's role and the workshop format*

The Instructors' Notes given below offer specific guidance on how to present the information, examples and exercises contained in each section of the manual. However, there are some general points about organising and presenting the content which you might find useful.

The teaching of each component of the *goal planning* (usually covered in one section of the manual) is based on the following format:

Information about the component
An example
An exercise for the trainee to try out
'Real life' practice in implementing the technique by working with a client

Information about each component is best presented by summarising the content of the section, and possibly presenting the main points using an overhead projector or other visual aid. We do not recommend reading the text aloud, or asking the trainees to read the section during the training session. It is better to encourage the trainees to read the manual in their own time and to use it for future reference.

The trainees should be asked to look at *the examples* in the appropriate section which should be used to draw attention to the important points about the aspect of *goal planning* highlighted in that section.

It is useful for the workshop to break up into small groups in order to try out *the exercises*. The instructor is then able to survey each group, and provide feedback and give assistance. On completing the exercise the group may be asked to present their results using the overhead projector [see 1(iv)]. In this way the whole workshop may benefit from further feedback.

The most valid 'test' in the development of the trainees' goal planning skills is their performance in the *'real life' practice* implementing the techniques by working with a client.

It is important at the beginning of training to direct the trainees to select a client with whom they will practise all the components of goal planning as the workshop progresses. In this way by the end of the workshop they will have a goal plan with one client fully prepared. Sometimes, trainees prefer to work on goal plans in pairs. This is perfectly acceptable, and can be very useful in institutional settings where the two trainees work opposite shifts and the goal plan involves day and evening behaviour (for example a personal self-help skill such as washing or dressing).

In a similar manner to the exercise work above, the results of trainees' practice in formulating components of the goal plan with clients are usefully presented to the workshop using an overhead projector.

It is very important to try and ensure that trainees have acquired the skills necessary in each component of the goal plan before moving on to the next section. This can only be done by allowing the trainees to practise the exercises. Their performance can then be assessed and appropriate feedback and further practice given.

Instructors' Notes for guiding trainees through the Sections of the Manual

Section 1

In some circumstances it may be necessary to adapt the content of the practical exercise in Section 1 (1.9).

In its presented format trainees would require time out from the workshop to complete 1.9. This would require introducing Section 1 on an additional day, prior to the training schedule suggested in 1(iii) in order to allow the trainees time to complete the exercise and return to the workshop for feedback. If this is not feasible due to time constraints we would suggest that you adopt one of the following alternatives:

● Introduce exercise 1.9 in Section 2, to be carried out for at least *one* of the behaviours listed in the Assessment Charts and assessed by the trainees.
● Present a video film of a client or clients performing a skill or task, and ask the trainees to use the record form in exercise 1.9 to pinpoint and record the filmed client behaviours. This is the method we have used in training and found to be successful.

Section 2

The section contains fairly brief information about the Assessment Charts and how they should be completed. It is important to refer the trainees to the information in Appendix II on how to complete the charts. You should emphasise their need to read Appendix II *before* commencing to complete the charts. In our experience trainees may neglect to *observe* client behaviours fully, relying on memory, the self report of the client or reports of other people. Consequently, we would advise you that you:

● Emphasise the need for objective and reliable observation.
● Ask the trainees to report back on exercise 2.5, with particular reference to 'own observations'.
● Allow the trainee sufficient time to make observational assessments (a week is often necessary).
● When teaching Section 7, check that the 'present client behaviour' in exercise 7.7 represents the *observed* behaviour of the client.

The authors have used video films of interviews with an elderly person and their chief carer to illustrate the following points in this section:

● Asking the client about items in the charts should be as informal as possible. Trainees should collect the information through several chats with the client rather than using a prolonged and formal question and answer session.
● The information reported by the client and their relative may not concur, and both sources may be subjective and unreliable. The need for *observation* may again be highlighted.

We have also used the films to familiarise trainees with the rating of the charts. This is done by asking them to complete the charts from information given in the films. The extra charts provided may be used for this purpose.

If you are unable to make and present videofilms, alternative suggestions are:

● Ask the trainees to complete the charts from their pooled knowledge of a client known to the majority of the group. This can be used to highlight discrepancies in their reports.
● Role play a client and/or relative and invite a trainee to interview you while the trainees fill in the charts from your responses.
● Spend time supervising the trainees' completion of the Charts in between workshop sessions.

Section 3

We have found it useful to allow trainees to practise completing a *strengths–needs list* prior to completing exercise 3.9 with a client.

This can be arranged using the assessment information recorded from the client as suggested in Section 2 above. Alternatively, you could present information about a client in a short handout. This could then be used by trainees to formulate a *strengths–needs list*.

The Master strengths–needs list provided may be copied for this purpose. This suggested additional exercise is best conducted in the small groups.

Section 4

Since the whole philosophy of the goal planning approach rests on the selection of *individual* needs, this section requires emphasis, particularly the practice selection of a need for the client with whom the trainee has selected to work. When giving feedback on exercise 4.5 check that the trainees have taken into account all the points in 4.3. In our experience trainees may neglect to take account of the practical considerations (4.3 (iii) and (iv)). Emphasise that although trainees may have selected an appropriate need when completing 4.5 in the workshop, it is essential that the selected need is discussed with the client after the training day. It may need to be modified when the client's wishes are considered.

You may be introducing goal planning into a very short-stay setting, for example, a short-stay hospital ward or rehabilitation unit. In this context, where the client's stay is less than the 5–6 weeks suggested for meeting needs (4.3 (iv)), it will be necessary to modify time periods.

Section 5

It is sometimes helpful to give a simple rationale for using clear behavioural language in writing goals (and the steps towards goals, Section 7). Staff may feel that the emphasis on doing so is unduly finicky. Explanations such as: 'In order to change behaviour, you have first to decide exactly what it is you want the client to achieve', can be helpful.

Check carefully the progress of the trainees in using clear behavioural language in exercises 5.2 and 5.3. Introduce further exercises of your own if the procedure has not been acquired.

Section 6

Trainees must learn how to integrate the client's strengths into the goal plans. Otherwise you will be in danger of producing standard recipes for change, rather than individualised plans.

Encourage trainees to 'brainstorm' as many relevant approaches as possible. At the same time, in exercise 6.3 check that the approaches are potentially *relevant to the goal*.

Section 7

In our experience, some trainees find breaking the goals into steps a particularly difficult skill to master. Common initial errors are:

● Writing steps in unclear or 'fuzzy' language.
● Confusing *steps* (what the client will be doing when the step is achieved) with *instructions (how* the step will be achieved see Section 8).

Our suggested timetable (see page 71) reflects the need to spend a relatively lengthy time period practising writing steps. Repeatedly reminding trainees that the *steps* should look like *goals* is useful. That is, they should contain 'who will be doing what, when and with how much help'.

Section 8
As with Section 7 we suggest you allow sufficient space in the timetable for exercises 8.13 and 8.14 to be rehearsed and adequate feedback given.

● It is useful to ask trainees if they would be able to carry out another trainee's step in exactly the same way as someone else given the written instructions on the Progress Chart.
● Make sure trainees understand how to set and interpret the *criterion of success*. Ask questions to check their understanding, for examle: 'If your criterion was 4/5 and your client achieved success on 3/5 occasions, which outcome would you tick?'

Section 9
This section allows time to re-emphasise the importance of using clear behavioural language. Introduce further practice for those trainees who have had difficulty in using clear language in Sections 5, 7 and 8.

Section 10
Discussion of future goal planning meetings is a convenient time to make arrangements for the first weekly meeting (preferably to take place within one week following training).

We have used video film to illustrate a typical meeting. This is largely to try and create enthusiasm for the maintenance of the plans through the weekly meetings. It is superfluous to the acquisition of goal planning skills and may confidently be omitted.

Section 11
Acquisition of some basic concept of the 'Constructional Approach' is not essential to acquiring goal planning skills. The section may be omitted, although we have found the ideas are readily assimilated.

We have. conducted exercise 11.11 with the whole workshop, rather than breaking into small groups.

We would suggest that the key issues to highlight are contained in 11.4, 11.6 and 11.7. If you wish to read more about the constructional approach you may find the following articles useful:

Fleming, I., Barrowclough, C. and Whitmore, R. (1983). 'The constructional approach'. *Nursing Mirror,* June 8th, 21–23.
Schwartz, A. and Goldiamond, I. (1975). *Social Casework: The Behavioural Approach.* Columbia University Press.

3(i)   How to make an evaluation of your staff members' performance
The next few pages contain some written exercises which you can use to see whether your staff have successfully gained the skills necessary to carry out *goal planning*. We have already explained how the training format relies on staff showing their expertise on one section before moving on to another. This is done to make sure, as much as possible, that staff do not move on too soon and become confused or overwhelmed by the material. The evaluation exercises that follow will enable you to make sure that staff can write goal plans successfully before going on to being expected to do them.

We suggest that you ask each member of staff to complete the evaluation by themselves as soon as possible after the training has finished i.e. within two or three days. Three different forms are presented: A, B and C [3(iii)]. You can choose which one to use and perhaps keep the others for a later follow-up evaluation. Each form of the evaluation consists of a short piece of written information about a client. Trainees are then required to use this information to construct a *goal plan* for the client. This will involve going through all of the stages used in training. Blank forms are provided.

When the staff have completed the exercises, collect them in and use the scoring guidelines [3(iv)] to score them up. We have used these guidelines for all of our evaluations and statistical analysis has shown that they enable reliable evaluations to take place when scored by people who are competent in goal planning. By this we mean that two experienced people who use the guidelines to score up the same completed exercise can achieve the same result. If you adhere to the scoring guidelines you will be able to make a more objective evaluation of your staffs' performances than if you relied on your own judgement. (Further information about this is available from the authors.)

In our experience an average score of 2 is a useful way of distinguishing trainees who have learned the skills necessary for goal planning from those who haven't. Studying the evaluation will let you know whether a member of staff has 'passed' or 'failed' on particular skills, e.g. writing the goal plan or picking an appropriate need. Thus, it may be the case that although someone's overall score indicates that they are skilled, a further analysis shows that they have real difficulty on a particular part of goal planning.

We suggest that you think carefully about giving feedback to your trainees about their performance. Do so individually and without giving them their actual score. Be as positive as possible, emphasising their achievements (trainees' *strengths* in this instance) and gently indicate that they perhaps need further help on any parts where their performance was unsatisfactory. We do not expect this to arise very often but it may happen that trainees need a little extra tuition after the training has ended.

3(ii) How to 'score' the staff evaluation exercises

When you have collected in the written exercises you will need to evaluate them. This is often called 'rating' and involves measuring the actual content against a criterion. These criteria would usually be standardised so that they actually mean something in general rather than reflecting merely the particular opinions of an individual. In this case we have developed certain guidelines which you can use to rate the exercises. These guidelines [see 3(iv)] have been used by us to rate many such exercises.

The guidelines will enable you to rate the exercises and give them a score of between 0 and 4. They give specific details of what constitute errors or missing information which will help you in rating any particular part of the exercise. These scores can be placed on the evaluation sheet along with any additional comments you wish to make. As we mentioned earlier, we have used a score of 2 as a 'pass' mark.

3(iii) Client Assessment Information

1. Mr Harrop is an 80-year-old widower who was referred to the day centre by the social worker following a short stay in hospital after a routine operation. Nursing staff were worried that although cheerful during his stay, he became very low when his discharge time came near and he seemed reluctant to go back home. Mr Harrop lives alone in a council flat which he moved to two years ago from a larger house with a garden. He has difficulty walking long distances (more than half a mile) due to arthritis, and is unable to get to the local shops (a mile away). He had a car up to a year ago when he had to stop driving due to failing eyesight and has not used public transport for a good many years. All his friends live close to his old house (3 miles away). Two ex-neighbours still visit (about once a month). Apart from this his only visitor is his daughter who visits once a week, and who does his shopping and washing. A home help helps with heavy cleaning once a week and he enjoys her company. He has meals on wheels three times a week. Mr Harrop is completely self-caring apart from these supports, and is always clean and well dressed.

He complains that he gets lonely, and is frustrated that he cannot get out to see people and to do his own shopping. Because of his physical disability and his poor eyesight he can no longer do things that he used to enjoy, such as gardening, reading, going to the pub, going to football matches. He says that he gets bored at home and that this gets him down. He very much enjoys going to the day centre two days a week. He has made several friends there and is generally popular with staff and other clients and joins in with activities such as bingo. Staff have discussed goal planning with Mr Harrop and he says he will 'have a go'. His social worker has said that she will be willing to help.

2.   Mrs Phillips is a 76-year-old widow who was referred to the day centre by the psychogeriatrician. She had been diagnosed as having senile dementia. In the last year she had been increasingly forgetful. Her family reported that it was difficult to have a conversation with her since she wandered off the point, and that while once very houseproud her house had now become untidy. Similarly, her personal hygiene was poor since she neglected to wash her clothes regularly and washed herself infrequently. Consequently her daughter and son-in-law decided to have her live with them, and she had moved in six months ago. She has another daughter who lives locally who takes her to her house two afternoons a week. Mrs Phillips is physically in good health, has no difficulties walking and her eyesight is good but has difficulty hearing and in the last few months has stopped wearing her hearing aid. All the cleaning, cooking etc. is done by the daughter who says it is easier to do everything for her mother since she is frightened that she might 'overdo it' or hurt herself, and that she needs looking after. At home she dresses herself, and can wash and bath herself but neglects to do so unless reminded by the family. Her poor personal hygiene upsets her daughter and she has taken to washing her mother herself. In the last month or so Mrs Phillips has taken to leaving the house and has been found wandering in the street where she used to live. Old neighbours have asked her in and given her a cup of tea, but this wandering has also upset the daughter and she has taken to locking her in the house.

As at home, she spends most of the time at the day centre dozing in the chair or walking restlessly up and down, sometimes walking out and having to be brought back by staff. Staff have found she is able to knit, and can wash up without much assistance. She is rarely spoken to by other clients. She used to be a very sociable woman, who enjoyed going to her local over 60s club where she would play the piano, and join in the singing and old-time dancing. She used to enjoy handicrafts such as knitting, sewing etc. Her daughter says she is willing to try out any advice staff suggest when goal planning was discussed with her.

3.   Mrs Stevens is an 82-year-old woman who has just moved into an elderly persons' home. Her husband died two year ago. For the last few years she has had several physical handicaps, following a stroke and a heart attack. Her husband did many of the domestic chores when he was alive, although Mrs Stevens always did the cooking and the light cleaning.

Following her husband's death, Mrs Stevens was very low and began to neglect her self-care and looking after the house. She had previously managed to get around in the house and as far as the local shops with the aid of the stick. Since Mr Stevens died she became more and more chair-bound and said that she did not want to attempt to go out. Her daughter visited daily, and with her encouragement Mrs Stevens would wash and dress herself. However, her daughter did all the housework, washing and preparation of meals. Her daughter felt that it was her duty to do this and that her mother needed to rest. Mrs Stevens had a good friend who visited daily. She enjoyed reading to this woman (Mrs Stevens eyesight was good), since her friend was partially sighted.

Mr and Mrs Stevens used to go to the local over 60s club regularly, and enjoyed playing cards there, and chatting to other members. They were also regular churchgoers.

It was decided that Mrs Stevens should move to the home when her daughter became unable to visit due to her own ill health. During her first few weeks at the home, it has been noticed that Mrs Stevens tends to avoid other residents and stayed in her room for long periods. She has not contacted her friend, and has no visitors apart from her daughter. She says she is lonely. She is neglecting her self care by not washing regularly and needs a lot of verbal prompting to make any light snacks for herself (cooked meals are provided). However, she is beginning to get on well with a couple of members of staff and has said that she will 'have a go' at goal planning.

3(iv) Evaluation of goal planning components rating scale

For each of the components of *goal planning* please rate the subject's written responses on a 0 to 4 scale according to the following criteria. Please refer to the scoring guidelines handout for further definition of the terms 'correct' 'error' and 'missing'.

0 – Information entirely incorrect or completely missing.

1 – Poor response, e.g. more errors than correct information; or more information missing than supplied e.g. less than 50% of possible strengths/needs listed.

2 – Fair response, e.g. more correct information than errors, but more than one error made; some information missing, e.g. only 50–75% of possible strengths/needs listed.

3 – Good response, e.g. most information supplied (for example: more than 75% of possible strengths/needs listed and no more than one error. This category can also be used if the overall quality of the response makes up for a significant amount of missing information, e.g. although a significant detail is missing, no errors are contained in the details supplied.

4 – Excellent response. Virtually all necessary information supplied and no errors made. This category can also be used if the overall quality of the response makes up for a small amount of missing information, e.g. although a minor detail is missing, no errors are contained in the otherwise full information supplied.

GOAL PLANNING EVALUATION SHEET

Name

Date assessment completed

Goal planning component	Score 0–4	Comments
Strengths–needs list		
Selecting need from strengths–needs		
Stating need as a clear goal		
Using strengths to develop list of approaches		
Breaking goal down into steps		
Goal Plan Progress Chart		

PINPOINTING AND OBSERVING A CLIENT'S BEHAVIOUR

Behaviour to be observed

When and where

Observers

Behaviours to be observed	Observer				Observer			
	Date				Date			
	No help	Verbal prompt	Physical prompt	Unable to do	No help	Verbal prompt	Physical prompt	Unable to do
1								
2								
3								
4								
5								
6								
7								
8								

This is a **master copy page** and may be copied. Reproduced from Barrowclough & Fleming, *Goal planning with elderly people*. Copyright © 1985 Christine Barrowclough and Ian Fleming.

STRENGTHS-NEEDS LIST

Client   Date

Strengths	**Needs**
What the individual can do, what s/he likes to do, and other people who are willing to help	State these positively – what s/he should be doing

SELECTING A NEED FROM THE STRENGTHS-NEEDS LIST

Name of client

Need selected to work on

Reasons for selecting the need

STATING CHOSEN NEED AS A CLEAR GOAL

Name of client

NEED which you have chosen to work on with your client

Clear GOAL for your client to meet

USING STRENGTHS TO DEVELOP A LIST OF APPROACHES FOR THE CLIENT TO REACH HIS OR HER GOAL

Name   **Date**

Goal decided upon for client

Strength (from Strengths–Needs list)	**Approaches** (Strengths can provide more than one approach)

GOAL PLANNING SHEET

Client's name	Date

Present client behaviour

Client's goal

GOAL PLAN	Date achieved

GOAL PLAN PROGRESS CHART

OUTCOME Successful	Name of client
Continued Changed and continued	Goal planner's name
Abandoned	Week beginning

Final goal

This week's step in GOAL PLAN

Instructions

No. of trial	1	2	3	4	5	6	7	8	9	10
Date										
Performance										
Expected criterion of success										

ELDERLY PERSON'S ASSESSMENT CHART

Client's name

Age

Date of birth

Address

Assessor's name

Name of relatives etc. assisting with Assessment

Date completed

ASSESSMENT   Section 1

Please tick the most appropriate answer

SENSORY ABILITIES

Dentures   Has own teeth

              Has dentures

Eyesight   Can see (or can see with glasses)

              Partially blind

              Totally blind

Hearing   No hearing difficulties without hearing aid

              No hearing difficulties, though requires hearing aid

              Has hearing difficulties which interfere with communication

MOBILITY

Walking   No difficulty in walking

              Walks unsteadily without aid or uses stick

              Walks only with aid (frame, tripod) or physical assistance

              Unable to walk and chairbound/bedfast

Stairs   Able to go up and down stairs independently

              Able to go up and down stairs with physical assistance or handrail

              Unable to go up and down stairs

Ability to go out of house   Able to use public transport independently

              Able to shop locally, visit neighbours etc. independently

              Unable to leave house unless accompanied

Frequency of leaving house   Gets out of house regularly (at least once a week)

              Gets out of house infrequently (at least once a month)

              Never or rarely gets out of house (less than once a month)

SOCIAL CONTACTS

Visits others, or has visitors regularly (every day)

Visits others or has visitors (at least once a week)

Visits others or has visitors rarely (once a month or less)

Please specify regular social contacts:

ASSESSMENT   Section 2(a)

Please tick the most appropriate column

PERSONAL SELF-HELP SKILLS

	Can do without help or supervision	Can do with minimum help or supervision	Requires maximum help or supervision	No opportunity to find out or observe
1 Undressing/dressing				
Completely dresses self, including difficult fastenings (e.g. zips, buttons)				
Completely undresses self, including difficult fastenings				
Dresses self in sensible sequence (e.g. does not put shoes on before socks)				
2 Selection of clothing				
Selects own clothes from drawer or wardrobe				
Chooses clothing and footwear appropriate to occasion (e.g. bed, shopping and weather conditions)				
3 Use of Toilet				
* Toilets self (daytime)				
* Toilets self (night-time)				
Wipes self, flushes toilet and adjusts clothing				
4 Personal Hygiene				
Washes hands and face when needed (e.g. in morning, after toilet, etc.)				
Has bath or shower when needed				
Attends to oral hygiene				
Washes hair				
Combs or brushes hair				
Shaves				
Changes underwear and socks/stockings/tights regularly				
5 Eating				
Uses knife, fork and spoon appropriately				
Table habits acceptable (e.g. no spilling, eats at a correct speed, etc.)				

* If incontinent, specify whether of urine or faeces or both

Specify frequency

ASSESSMENT   Section 2(b)

Please tick the most appropriate column

	Can do without help or supervision	Can do with minimum help or supervision	Requires maximum help or supervision	No opportunity to find out or observe
DOMESTIC SELF-HELP SKILLS				
Washes clothes by hand				
Washes clothes (by machine)				
Irons				
Makes hot drinks				
Makes simple snacks				
Makes cooked meals				
Sets and clears table				
Washes, dries and puts items away				
Makes bed				
Dusts				
Vacuums				
Cleans Windows				
SHOPPING AND HANDLING MONEY				
Shops for food and household needs				
Shops for other personal needs				
Pays bills, rent, collects pension				
Competent in handling money (can add coins together to pay and can check change)				
COMMUNICATION				
Understands what others say				
Is able to make self understood by others				
Writes letters or messages				
Uses telephone				
OCCUPATION				
Keeps self occupied with purposeful activities				
FIRST AID AND HEALTH				
Seeks medical help when required				
Takes medicines reliably				
Shows awareness of danger and exercises caution				
ORIENTATION AND MEMORY				
Knows full name, age, date of birth				
Knows approximate time, knows month, year				
Knows address				
Finds way about house				
Finds way about neighbourhood				
Recognises familiar people				
Can remember simple instructions				

EVALUATION OF GOAL PLANNING COMPONENTS SCORING GUIDELINES

Component	Full and correct information	Errors	Missing information
Strength/ Needs list	Virtually all (90%) strengths and needs given in CAI supplied. These should include significant important strengths such as the client is willing/keen to take part in *goal planning* or people who might help. Needs *must* be written in positive terms.	A need stated negatively.	Strengths and needs contained in CAI and not supplied. See Rating Scale for allocation of scores according to % missing information. See 'correct information' column for examples of what constitutes 'significant' information.
Selecting a need	Important to client; good chance of success; realistically can be achieved in short term.	Need selected due to importance to people other than client (e.g. institution relatives). N.B. this would constitute a serious error. Irrespective of other information supplied the response should not be given a score of greater than 2.	Information relevant to any of three guidelines listed under 'correct information' column not supplied.
Stating need as clear goal	*Who* (clients name) will be doing *what* (in terms of client's behaviours) *when* (at least in terms of frequency) and with *how much help.*	Goal not stated in terms of client's behaviours.	The *who, what, when* and *how much* help not supplied.
Using strengths to develop approaches	At least 4 strengths used to develop at least 4 approaches *relevant* to chosen goal.	Approach completely unrelated to the goal chosen.	Less than 4 strengths used; less than 4 approaches developed. Guideline: 3 strengths/approaches = 3 2 strengths/approaches = 2 1 strength/approach = 1
Goal plan	Final goal and steps state *who, what, how.* Final goal gives *when* (see above). No fuzzies. Relevant present client behaviour supplied. At least 3 steps given. Realistic gap(s) between steps, leading naturally to final goal.	Fuzzies. Irrelevant present client behaviour. Unrealistic gap(s) between steps. Incomplete, e.g. doesn't lead to final goal. Confuses 'instructions' with 'steps' (see below).	Present client behaviour not supplied (completely missing is significant; incomplete is minor).
Progress chart	Final goal and step give *who, what, when, how.* Instructions are in clear behavioural language and state *who, what, when* and *how* for goal planner. Includes instruction to complete boxes and gives criterion of success.	Fuzzies. Instructions confused with breaking goal down into steps.	*Who, what, when* or *how* missing from goal, step or instructions. No instruction to complete boxes. No criterion of success.